California Houses of

Gordon Drake

The Malibu House (additional pictures on pages 72-75.)

Douglas Baylis and Joan Parry

*with new preface by Glenn Murcutt
and new introductory essay by Pierluigi Serraino*

California Houses of
Gordon Drake

Copyright 2011

William Stout Publishers
Printed in China

Contents

Preface *by Glenn Murcutt* — i

Gordon Drake: A California Modernist of Intent — vi
   by Pierluigi Serraino

About This Book *by George A. Sanderson* — 7

Proem — 9

1. **The Islands**: *five years of war* — 11
2. **Los Angeles**: *the west* — 15
3. **Los Angeles**: *the city* — 23
4. **The Sierra** — 27
5. **Los Angeles**: *the houses* — 31
6. **Carmel**: *the big dream* — 46
7. **Carmel**: *the cold facts* — 51

8. **San Francisco** — 67

Appreciations — 79

   by Carl Birger Troedsson — 81

   by Harwell Hamilton Harris — 83

   by Walter L. Doty — 85

Acknowledgments — 87

Working Drawings of Gordon Drake — 88

Index — 91

i

Introduction

Glenn Murcutt

As an eleven year old and the eldest of five children, I was introduced to architecture through my builder-father's subscriptions to a number of North American journals including Architectural Forum, Architectural Record and, I think, Progressive Architecture. By the time I was thirteen, I was familiar with the work of many architects. At the same time and during all the school holidays, reluctantly I was conscripted to working in my father's joinery shop where I learned much about timber and appropriate detailing including the fabrication of windows, doors, stairs, and the building of a racing sailing skiff, including all the stainless fittings. By seventeen I knew well the work of the Greene brothers, Wright, Maybeck, Irving Gill, the Keck brothers, Philip Johnson, the Weese brothers, Elliot Noyes, Craig Ellwood, Charles and Ray Eames, Schindler, Gordon Drake and a number of other luminaries from the U.S. Each architect's published work was required reading and questions to me were asked of each on the underlying design principles. All questions had to be intelligently answered otherwise I had to re-read the text.

Following the end of WWII, things were tight and buildings had to be economical. In the late 1940's and 50's neither Australia nor the US regarded air conditioning as a given, so many buildings were designed to be economical, having appropriate orientation, integrated sun control systems and thermal insulation. Many architects at the time recognized the importance of working with the site and not against the site; nature and climatic considerations again became serious considerations. These factors remain important in designing domestic architecture in Australia. Given the energy issues we all now face, it is worth looking back to the Case Study houses and also the work of Gordon Drake who, surprisingly, was not included in the elite and very good group of designers.

In 1947 when I was eleven years old, my father brought the house that Gordon Drake designed for himself in California to my attention. The memory of that publication has remained with me because Drake's work became the subject of lengthy discussions at home over subsequent years.

What I recall and what has remained of importance in the design of the Drake house was a plan so simple yet spacious beyond its size. I recall how the design separated the public and private use of space that started with a private terrace courtyard that had been formed by an excavation into the hillside. Drake achieved a logical design that was deceptively simple in a very small house. Full height paired doors were set below lowered eaves extending to form pergolas that projected over the terrace. The retention of mature native flora within the courtyard terrace provided an immediate mature landscape, allowing the house to comfortably nestle into its site the external space opened and connected to the hillside and beyond to reveal the higher landscape and the sky. The inclusion of nature and an organic relationship with the natural elements were always integral to Drake's thinking.

By working with the module, often around 1.8 meters, the design presented a logical, easily assembled structural system which resulted in the clarity and strength of design. The system also minimized the use of materials and labor and made for a most economical work pattern, a factor Drake regarded as very important in delivering quality architecture to many. The materials he used were simple; for structural components concrete and timber were used for floors, with timber for wall studs, supporting posts and roof beams, each being dimensioned for their relative loads and spans, all sourced, I believe, from within the USA. The establishment of the module set the position of dividing walls. The finishes were simple where internal timber surfaces were left clear and the external timbers protected with dark oil stain. Bricks were used for pavers for the entry, pond, and the full courtyard terrace area.

This high quality unpretentious work extended into Drake's small body of subsequently constructed work in what was a short professional life that ended tragically on the ski slopes.

I recall other fine works by Drake but his own house remains the most powerful in my memory; its quality was reinforced by extensive discussions over my adolescent years with my father Sydney Arthur Murcutt who would say 'look at this one, son, it's a beauty, simple, economical, liveable, and beautiful. Learn from it!' - and of course I did - and I think so did a number of Australian architects practicing in the mid-late fifties!

In an era besotted with computer generated and often extremely noisy 'architecture' where anything can be 'designed'...simply because it can...the reprinting of this book on Gordon Drake is a timely reminder that good design lasts.

Gordon Drake:
A California Modernist of Intent

Pierluigi Serraino

The architectural history of the twentieth century holds its share of celebrated protagonists whose lives were cut short at the peak of their creativity – for instance Italian rationalist Giuseppe Terragni died at 39, Polish American Matthew Nowicki at 40, Finnish master Eero Saarinen and Bauhaus guru Laszlo Moholy Nagy at 51, San Francisco architect Timothy Pflueger at 54, and Swedish master Erik Gunnar Asplund at 55. Few architects, however, have been as prolific and innovative as Gordon Drake (American 1917-1952) in the remarkably short time he lived. With Drake, who was barely 34 years old when he died in a ski accident at a Sierra resort in Northern California on January 15, 1952, the tragedy of his death stands out as intensely as the exceptional depth of his work. During his compressed professional trajectory, Drake achieved a body of work enviable to much older colleagues both in quality and quantity. Furthermore, the apparent spontaneity of Drake's output finds virtually no rivals in the annals of modern architecture. His designs were magnets of media attention: they were generously published in the national and international press, and they earned Drake a deluge of awards in the course of his meteoric seven-year career. Although most of his work is in California – with the exception of projects in Hawaii executed during his United States Marine Corps service; the unbuilt Noble house in Ann Arbor, Michigan; prototypical designs such as the "expandable house" for the Woman's Home Companion; and demonstration projects in Sunset magazine – Drake's standing was broadcast nationally during his lifetime. His design legacy was a critical inspirational reference in the early work of contemporary masters, including Pritzker prize winners Glenn Murcutt and Frank Gehry. And yet, too few practitioners, historians, and design aficionados know of Drake. It is worthwhile, then, to reconsider the merits of his architecture nearly sixty years after his demise.

Drake created a new architecture that was embraced by postwar middle-class America and did not abandon the rigor of modernism. He revamped the ailing homegrown design vocabulary of wood architecture amidst the growing paradigm of steel and glass construction for residential design. With its distinctive spatiality and strong regional tone, Drake's architectural imagery provided a third alternative to the irreconcilable division in postwar American architecture between its grassroots heritage – exemplified by the Gregory farmhouse in Santa Cruz, Northern California, designed in 1926-7 by William Wilson Wurster – and the ideological celebration of industrial technology hailed by the European masters transplanted on American soil – most notably Walter Gropius and Mies Van der Rohe and epitomized by the Case Study House #8 in Pacific Palisades, Southern California, designed in 1945-9 by Charles Eames. Drake merged the regionalist pledge to anchor architecture to its site with the modernist assertion that design disengaged from the industrial processes of mass production was a proposition with neither relevance nor a future in avant-garde design discourse. Instead of exploring the expressive potential of structural steel, as did many early modernist designers, Drake retained plywood as his primary building material, though he did use modern prefabricated methods. Plywood's exceptional performance for military products in wartime and the great abundance of Douglas Fir growing in Northern California made it the perfect bridge material for resolving the design conflicts between regionalist militants and dogmatic modernists. It appealed to both those attached to traditional building materials and values and the growing catalog of young modern voices in postwar American architecture. The strength, lightness, and adaptability of plywood in the service of residential design for the masses distinguished Drake's work and earned him attention on the stage of the domestic press.

Despite his allegiance to wood, Drake's work also demonstrates innovative attributes typically associated with the machine aesthetic and the modern concept of

Haleakala Theatre, Maui

the architect as a problem-solver. The lessons he absorbed from the mechanization of architecture include the following: activation of exterior and interior walls with moving screens and slides; use of classic floor-to-ceiling glass openings; strategic placement and orientation of structures on the land to best harness natural resources; and use of the latest in home appliances and amenities. Drake's engagement with modernist design, however, passed over its dogmatic character. Rather, he combined modernist qualities and approaches with deliberate simplicity and warmth, producing house designs that were at once compatible and consistent with traditional middle-class American values and prototypes for modern living. He upheld the hearth as the core of domestic space, and a formal plainness made his work more accessible and easy on the untrained eye. Drake also understood well the connections among design, site, and habitation, and through his frequent contributions to shelter magazines such as Sunset, House & Garden, and Better Homes & Gardens, he educated middle-class Americans in matters of design and comforted their anxiety when facing choices for their domestic environment – choices between the "sleeks" of modern architecture and the stylistic hodgepodge of Beaux-Arts mansions.

The demobilization of the trained workforce from Eisenhower's military-industrial complex to peacetime occupations and the conversion of the country's wartime physical infrastructure into civilian production machines in support of the postwar society and economy generated a cult of the present, of the here and now, and in California, especially, that deeply affected all cultural discourses. The hardliners of the modernist camp staunchly believed in this celebration of the present; Drake's work, on the other hand, did not wholly break from the past. He embraced America's romantic call of the land, a metaphor referencing the settlement of the western frontier and mythologized by historians such as Frederick Jackson Turner (1861-1932). The honesty associated with raw organic materials such as unpainted wood combined with simple construction and a lack of ornamentation presented the general public with an architecture of unadorned beauty that recalled the humble bungalow in the Arts and Crafts tradition and straightforward wood framing. Furthermore, his architecture offered an economically viable solution to meet the rising demand for single-family housing in the immediate postwar years by using available technology and a sophisticated yet unintimidating design idiom. While Harwell Hamilton Harris (one of Drake's mentors) and Mario Corbett (a contemporary Northern California maverick) independently devised thoroughly modern wood-based design idioms for contemporary living at the higher end, Drake used the same materials to design houses within budgets available to returning veterans who were eager to build homes and celebrate their newfound stability. The work read new and familiar, autochthonous to California whether north or south. It was both easy to sell to the lay audience and resilient enough to counter the pervasive skepticism about technology in the building industry – for instance, precision hardware and materials with high dimensional stability and minimal tolerances.

Drake's remarkable synthesis of familiar materials and direct building methods is manifest in the variety of systematic and efficient planning modules he used. The modules ranged from 2' 8" for the Noble House in Ann Arbor, Michigan; 3' for kitchens and garden layouts; and 4' for the Hanna, Presley, Martin, and Wallace houses – all in Los Angeles. Drake's design modules create a regular pattern of alternating areas of shade and light that correspond to the fenestration and exterior soffits. This spatial rhythm of broken light is fully integrated with the overall open plan design. Clerestory windows, entire facades opening to patios, sheltered outdoor areas, slender footprints, and expansive views both from inside out and within the houses, along with simple wood materials and processes gave Drake's residential designs an entirely new flavor, one thoroughly consistent with the imperatives of the postwar dweller. Even brick paving, which was anathema to the palette of the modernist architect, frequently appears in Drake's projects and transcends nostalgic references to rural vernacular.

While such materials certainly appealed to the more organic strands of postwar America, they also unquestionably denied Drake's entry into the pages of Arts &

Architecture, the legendary Los Angeles-based magazine which launched the iconic Case Study House program in January 1945. Managing editor John Entenza (1903-1984) was the gatekeeper to the canon of a particular notion of modernity in Southern California: one steeped in the unwavering adoption of war technologies to peacetime design and prosperity. If Charles Eames was the ideal soldier and designer-in-action of this vision, then Gordon Drake was its antithesis. He definitely did not support Entenza's advocacy of machine-based technology and dismissal of an architecture with pitched roofs. Unfortunately, exclusion from Entenza's circle of favorites impeded the aspiring modernist architect's national repute and opportunities for middle-class commissions.

By the time Drake left Los Angeles for Northern California in mid-1948, more than a dozen Case Study houses had been built or fully designed. Presumably, he was familiar with the program and may have even visited several of the houses. Likely wanting to separate himself from the LA milieu of Entenza and the Case Study House designers, Drake moved first to Carmel in 1948 and then to San Francisco in 1950, where he established a private practice. Independent in thought and committed to working within the wood idiom steadfastly unsupported by the design elite of Southern California, Drake embarked on a quest for an architecture rooted in natural materials. His undated "plan of work" for an unfunded application to a Guggenheim fellowship reads: "The broad purpose of the study will be to explore how these inter-

Hanna House, Los Angeles

related factors [land, orientation, wind, weather, and others] may be better employed and integrated to produce an improved condition for family life."[1] The exploration and actualization of the intimate relation of the house to its site defines the ideological program of Gordon Drake's architecture.

Drake worked alone. In a recent interview Clinton Ternstrom, a Los Angeles architect and a former student colleague of Drake's at the University of Southern California (USC), reminisced about him: "He was never a joiner … ever, ever."[2] In fact, Drake was a solo player in private practice, working only with occasional project-based employees. Ternstrom further noted: "He was non-collaborative because he was driven and wanted to express himself, and he could do it without aid. He did not want the counterpart. As a result he never did big commercial work."[3] Ternstrom's memories go back to the formative years at USC, when the latter's more private personality was already evident, and so, too, was his inner turmoil and unsettling dissatisfaction with the current state of architecture, which he expressed in personal letters and private exchanges with his mentors and closest friends and would permeate his brief path as an architect. Architect Maggie Baylis characterized Drake's outlook and experiences as a "struggle … fraught with human searching."[4] She shared this assessment with Drake's mother, Pearl Drake Hunter, in a letter about the monograph on Drake – the only monographic study of Drake's work – that her husband and professional partner, San Francisco landscape architect Douglas Baylis, prepared with writer Joan Parry.

Born in Texas on March 19, 1917, Gordon Drake was raised in California during the Depression years. In Goals for America, an exploratory study commissioned in 1942 by the Twentieth Century Fund, the author Stuart Chase identified priorities the United States would need to establish once World War II ended. In the early part of the publication, Chase describes the moral, social, and financial climate in the dramatic decade following the 1929 stock market crash and ensuing economic collapse. The loss of confidence in the nation-state and its institutions and values in the aftermath of that catastrophe significantly altered the American concept of citizenship and longstanding culture of self-affirmation. Traditional ways of thinking about economic revitalization were useless because of the historically unprecedented conditions the nation fell into. Most significant was the shattering of the psychological security that the American people had nurtured in the strength of the economic system.

From census reports and site visits performed by university researchers and government representatives in various states, it became absolutely clear to the political powers that housing was the number one priority in the imminent and extreme makeover of postwar America. Chase wrote: "I think we can take it as demonstrated that the budget will call for somewhere between a million and two million dwelling units, over the whole country, every year, for at least ten years after the war ends. That will make the biggest single demand upon manpower of any project on the horizon – the largest pool for postwar work."[5] Not surprisingly, speed of construction became the operational imperative in a building industry that when compared to other manufacturing sectors in the country was lagging behind in processes and practices. However, the long-standing tradition of handicraft prevailed in that sector, and therefore the application of assembly line methods for production encountered strong resistance from the unions for decades; laborers feared job losses to the exclusive benefit of the industrial aristocracy. Nonetheless, prefabrication, fast assembly, and the use of light frames sheathed with plywood established the basis for the new era in housing design. Such intense rationalization of the construction process was a cost-saving measure, for sure, but also the only viable way to meet record demand.

It is worthwhile noting that the accelerated production of goods supported by new processes and applications in wartime America – a program driven by self-preservation and a unity of purpose that World War II engendered in the American people – transpired in plain view of two German modern masters, Mies van der Rohe and Walter Gropius, who were both living in the United States at that time. The extraordinary collective human effort they witnessed strongly defined the architectural scene Drake entered upon his release from military duty. Drake's architectural journey, however, had actually begun a decade earlier. In 1937 he enrolled in the architecture program at USC, from which he graduated in 1941. In those early days Drake the student was a good conversationalist, but to the best of Ternstrom's recollection, "he did not seem to show promise! Gordon was trying to find his way. He was not a thinker then, but he was striving in that direction, searching, attempting to think things out instead of sketching until the problem was solved."[6] The very first impression he gave was outright unflattering: "I knew him as a loud mouth kind of odd guy. I just saw him in the patio horsing around and found out that like another friend of mine he was an athlete, a hurdler. And I thought here is just another athlete. Most of them did not amount to a damn. Their interests were elsewhere. Gordon had an engaging personality once you got to know him. He had a good physique, he wasn't tall, but he had a funny way about him, and he was talking seriously about architecture."[7] That architecture was important to Drake was clear to him from his initial coursework. Architecture was to be an instrument of betterment and intensification of living: rather than a house sitting on a piece of property, Drake envisioned permeable enclosures for the improvement of the human condition. Drake himself wrote words to this effect: "Youth has learned to recognize that contemporary architecture represents a way of living that transforms the home from the role as mere shelter to the center of existence. Architects capable of making this possible must work toward this end as one phase of their practice."[8]

Two figures changed the course of events for Drake during his college years. The first individual was Carl Birger Troedsson, a Swedish professor and architect who taught at USC. Of Troedsson, Ternstrom notes: "He was the first man who had a forward looking sense of developing architecture. He taught third or fourth year. And I would say that that was one of the greatest influences on Gordon's life, on his thinking. And he also influenced Ed Killingsworth. Troedsson was a modernist, and he influenced quite a few students. He was very stern, wasn't an outgoing man, but he was a good teacher for those who meshed with him. Gordon became a good student, he didn't do outstanding work, but he was a serious student, which was a remarkable change."[9] Troedsson's sensibilities to climate, local materials, and a socially oriented modernism derived from his homeland Sweden, which, like California, has a mostly temperate climate and substantial forests of spruce, pine, and birch. Arriving in California in the later 1930s, Troedsson undoubtedly experienced the Stockholm International Exposition designed by Erik Gunnar Asplund in 1930 and paramount to introducing modern architecture to Sweden. At this fair, Troedsson would have also encountered the work of architect Sven Markelius, whose projects defined Swedish modernist housing design. Characterized by standardization and concerns for land-use policies, high quality, and affordability, Swedish modernism sought to upgrade the national infrastructure. It also took advantage of local materials – namely wood and brick – foregoing the preferred steel and glass of most European modernist design because these materials had to be imported. Coming from this background, Troedsson instilled in Drake an unconditional commitment to the socially oriented tenets of modern architecture.

The second influential figure on Drake was Harwell Hamilton Harris, from whom the young designer absorbed a unique sensitivity to wood detailing and the tectonic aspects of architecture. Drake was a draftsman for Harris between 1939 and 1941, a period during which Harris designed and constructed what is arguably his masterpiece, the Weston Havens house in Berkeley, California, completed on December 8, 1941, the day after the attack on Pearl Harbor. During his time in Harris' office, Drake internalized the senior architect's expressive treatment of panels and preference for plywood, fiberboard, and cement board.

As a Marine Corps engineer, Drake "supervised the construction of roads, air-

Interior of the Drake House in Los Angeles

fields, and military installations."[10] Combined, his technical expertise and design talent sparked a very rich creative season lasting from his return from war through the late forties. In 1946 alone, Drake designed about a dozen houses of which only a few were built. Many of these single-family houses were one level, though occasionally two, and whenever possible he engaged prefabrication processes. Though he was primarily a practitioner, Drake spent 1947-8 as a visiting critic in architecture at his alma mater, USC, where he lectured in third, fourth, and fifth year design courses. Ternstrom was surprised to see how much Drake had matured since his student days: "Our paths didn't cross until probably after the war. I lost track of Gordon. Then the next recollection, I don't know how we met again, but he just said 'Come on up! I just finished my house.' And it is just over here, a few canyons away. I was struck by it. I really was. I had seen drawings and designs, but they did not reflect something I am very sympathetic [to]. I don't like stiff, stark design. His was a lovely little simple thing; with a brick floor.... I was just so pleased to see Gordon come along those lines. It was very difficult for him though, because all of us struggled for clients, and I knew he was going to have a tough time like all of us and I didn't hear too much of him until his work was being published. By then he had moved up north. And there again I recognized that his work was going to be outstanding. Gordon then just vanished until I picked up the [Los Angeles] Times one morning and read that he had gone skiing and never came back. Another career stopped short."[11]

Drake's own house (10433 Oletha Lane, Los Angeles, California) completed in 1946 represents his holistic approach to architecture. Published in various articles of the time, it was labeled the "basic house" and "minimum dwelling" – names indicative of Drake's attempt to redefine the ABC's of postwar living in terms other than the tenets outlined in the research on optimal dwellings by German modernists Heinrich Tessenow, Walter Gropius, and Ludwig Hilberseimer, among others. Drake's house is an example of environmental consciousness with its compact, minimal footprint – and yet it offers a spacious feeling. It is the way that the residence sits on the land that makes this project groundbreaking in its disarming simplicity. With its long axis oriented north-south, the rectangular planned Drake house rests serenely on a sheet of brick pavers laid in a basket weave pattern. Conscious of the growing postwar car culture, Drake's design for this house – and all other subsequent ones – includes a carport prominently situated near the main entrance. Moving past the Drake house carport and through the foyer entrance, one takes three turns to eventually enter the main living space – kitchen, bathroom, and built-in elements – which divides the structure into public and private quarters. A parade of majestic double doors along the west side of the main living spaces opens up the interior to a vast outdoor area that doubles the home's square footage by pushing living functions out to the exterior. The roof, sloping gently toward the west, extends the sightlines outward without any loss of privacy. Climate control motivated many of Drake's design decisions and material selections, from the indoor-outdoor living spaces to the placement of the building on its site, the exterior sheathing, and the structural assemblies. Interestingly, the Drake house embodies many of the principles behind what is known today as evidence-based design, which correlates architectural design and health. And finally, his own home design incorporated lightweight, moveable light screens to support greater flexibility, a strategy for improving the viability of domestic architecture emerging in the postwar period. Indeed, many of the key characteristics of Drake's architecture are present in this early project.

With the 1947 Spillman house, located in Los Angeles, Drake extends his design concepts to a two-story scheme sitting on an uneven site. Situating the entrance on the lower level of the structure, he scripts an ingenious sequence of events where architecture, hardscape, and landscape are completely fused into a single coherent statement. Inside, Drake arranges the four main spaces – the entry/dining room, living room, kitchen, and bedroom – as a chess-like exercise, producing imaginative solutions to otherwise compressed spaces. His alternative iterations of the relationship between the core living spaces and the shell of the structure reinforce the strength and malleability of the initial concept – a compact and spacious living unit. He activates the cross section of the house with skillful integration of modular planning, light screens, plywood construction, and indoor and outdoor areas, and thereby transforms the residential cell of the 1946 "basic house" (Drake's house) into a larger edifice.

With the Presley house in Los Angeles, also completed in 1947, Drake pushes the idea of prefabrication for mass housing to a new level of architectural expression. The design incorporates interchangeable parts that allow the house to morph into many different layouts to accommodate changing family needs. Stressed-skin plywood panels measuring 4'x8' and arranged on a 4' square module establish regularity in the architectural character and rationality in the house construction. The spaciousness of the Presley design remained consistent with Drake's previous projects. One enters the house from the garage, which is situated perpendicular to the longitudinal axis of the house. Along that axis, or "spine," both public areas and private quarters are equally supplied with generous outdoor terraces.

The "unit house," built in 1950 in Hayward, California, a suburban community located east of San Francisco, demonstrates Drake's continued interest in designing flexible homes that evolve as needed. The three-stage expansion program he envisioned for this project yields unified architectural images and integrates a variety of outdoor spaces. It also demonstrates Drake's ongoing efforts to achieve stylistic simplicity and unity through economical processes. For instance, the 6' modular system, legible in the exterior paving, confers friendly discipline to the overall design of the "unit house." The gable roof, though it appears to simply mimic the popular roofline of the day, further contributes to Drake's careful orchestration of design, process, and materials in the way it allows light to create an assertive organizational axis inside the home.

Berns House, Malibu

Media exposure was Drake's most effective line of attack in his unrelenting self-promotional campaign. There is something uncanny about how meticulously he entered the names of magazine editors, photographers, and architectural writers into his personal notebooks. While all other names (e.g., clients and contractors) are hastily handwritten, those related to the press world were typed and perfectly spaced and aligned. Little did these media professionals know that they were accomplices to Drake's own personal PR project. Drake's precocious understanding of "publish to flourish" – the golden ticket to twentieth century architecture – began with a serendipitous encounter with legendary architectural photographer Julius Shulman of Los Angeles in 1946, who became Drake's most loyal ally. When asked about their initial meeting during an interview, the master photographer could not remember the circumstances that brought them together. Nonetheless the admiration and affection that he nurtured for Drake was unconditional: "Had he lived until he was 50 he would have been a grand master."[12] Shared personality traits and experiences (they both were young athletes) certainly provided common ground over which Drake and Shulman bonded.

Shulman photographed six Drake projects, five of which were located in Los Angeles: Drake's own house (1946), the Rucker house (April 1947), the Presley house (July 1947), the Damman house (1950), and the Berns house (1953). The sixth one was the Scribner house (1951), known as the "unit house." In recording these projects Shulman turned out some of the most arresting compositions of California modernism and helped promote Drake's work. About the work Shulman recalled: "Drake was always around me, we worked together. He was not controlling on the photo shoot."[13] Following the photographic assignment of Drake's personal residence, Shulman encouraged him to submit the project to competitions sponsored by American Home and Progressive Architecture. A great many design awards ensued to Drake's professional benefit.

Shulman's photographs illustrated the earliest publications of Drake's work (1947). In the photographs, Shulman beautifully captured the "simplistic romance," as he liked to say, embodied in Drake's architectural vision. Though designed with minimal resources, Drake's homes appeared every bit high-end through the lens and stage mastery of Shulman. Using the same bag of tricks that had won him worldwide popular acclaim, Shulman recorded Drake's projects with people and carefully orchestrated compositions. In a photograph of his own home, Drake poses with his staff, a niece of the photographer, and David Presley, a future client. Esther McCoy, architectural attaché to the Case Study program and California modernism, posed on the brick patio (at left) for a picture of the Berns house in Malibu that made the cover

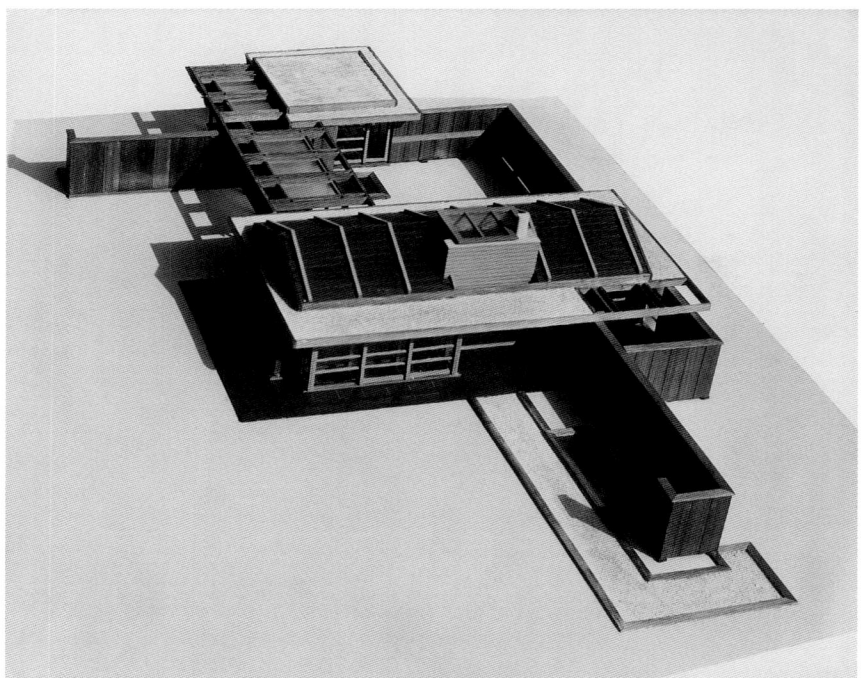

School of Architecture, Monterey (unbuilt)

of Sunset magazine.

Drake changed his office address in almost erratic fashion during his seven-year practice, a symptom of his private turbulence, anxiety, and restlessness. Some of his drawing sets are inscribed 1231 Malcom Street in West Los Angeles. Other early documents are signed under MADAC Design Associates, an acronym for Modern Architecture Design and Construction, with an address of 19433 Oletha Lane, Los Angeles. Another address recorded for MADAC is 10438 Oletha Lane, Los Angeles. He then appears as Gordon Drake at 4201 Sunset Boulevard, Los Angeles. Relocating in 1948 to Monterey Bay, his office contact became simply Box 2905, Carmel, California. He eventually landed at 619 Washington Street, San Francisco, an office space he shared with landscape architect Douglas and architect/graphic designer Maggie Baylis. What is interesting is that in spite of this constant moving and his anxiety, Drake's architecture was being published routinely in Europe alongside the leading architects of the time, most of whom were at least twenty years older than Drake.

While in the monograph on Drake that Doug and Maggie Baylis published in the 1950s it mentions that he wanted to establish a school of architecture in Monterey, the real motivations for his departure to Northern California are unknown. However,

Berns House, Malibu

it is likely that financial stress and a lawsuit in Carmel contributed to his decision to move on. In fact, in a letter written to Maggie Baylis not long after Drake's death, Pearl Drake Hunter mentioned that this legal entanglement – of which there are no details readily available in what is left of his archive – wrecked her son's spirit. Brief correspondence found in the archives of William Wilson Wurster, then Dean of the School of Architecture at the University of California, Berkeley, shows that Drake applied for a position of lecturer of architectural design there.[14] In his letter dated April 24, 1950, to the acting dean Professor Raymond Jeans, he wrote: "The primary reason for my interest is that I feel every effort should be made by the men actively engaged in practice to relate the knowledge they have gained to the students in the architectural schools."[15] Compared to the Los Angeles years, those in San Francisco presented far fewer design opportunities; Drake's only projects of note built between 1949 and 1951 were the "unit house" for the Scribners in Hayward, the Berns house in Malibu, and the townhouse for Doug and Maggie Baylis in San Francisco. This professional demise paralleled the emotional decline of Gordon Drake.

What was Gordon Drake's influence on his contemporaries? This question is difficult to answer given the short duration of his professional practice, though his impact must have been felt nationally as well as internationally as a result of the many articles on his work that were published during his life in journals ranging from the Italian Domus to the French L'Architecture d'Aujourd'hui, and of course in the most highly regarded American journals. Interviews and reminiscences by those who knew him reveal a young designer who was deeply convinced that architecture was a vehicle for individual and social reform.

What is the significance of Gordon Drake today? The answer is fourfold: his legacy comprises his understanding of 1) the relationship between construction methods and design language, 2) the environmental impact of architecture, 3) the expressive potential and flexibility of modular planning, and 4) the social responsibility of the architect. From his youthful vantage point and with a discerning nature, Drake saw the dangers of an architecture wasteful in construction and lacking a sensitivity to nature, human values, and financial constraints. He anticipated, sixty years ago, the environmental threats we are presently facing by promoting the use of local materials and incorporating site-specific climatic and topographic conditions into designs. Thus, despite the six decades that separate his death from the current generation, Drake's values and ideas persist in some of the most pressing architectural issues and trends of our time.

I am deeply indebted to my friends Alan Hess and Barbara Lamprecht for sharing their knowledge on the subject and giving me critical feedback in the writing of this essay, and to Carrie McDade for her untiring commitment to the beauty of the English language.

Notes
1. Drake, G. Plan of Work, Guggenheim Fellowship, n.d. Gordon Drake Papers, Richmond, California.
2. Clinton Ternstrom, in discussion with the author, September 9, 2007.
3. Ibid.
4. Maggie Baylis to Pearl Drake Hunter, 18 September 1955, Gordon Drake Papers, Richmond, California.
5. Chase, S. Goals for America. A Budget of our Needs and Resources. Guidelines to America's future as reported to the Twentieth Century Fund. New York, 1942, p. 58.
6. Clinton Ternstrom, in discussion with the author, September 9, 2007.
7. Ibid.
8. Drake, G. "Modular house on Pacific coast capitalizes on the area's famous topography, climate and materials." Architectural Forum 87, no. 3 (1947): 110.
9. Clinton Ternstrom, in discussion with the author, September 9, 2007.
10. Resume of Gordon Drake, n.d. Gordon Drake Papers, Richmond, California.
11. Clinton Ternstrom, in discussion with the author, September 9, 2007.
12. Julius Shulman, in discussion with the author, September 9, 2007.
13. Ibid.
14. William Wilson Wurster to Gordon Drake, 15 January 1951, Records of the College of Environmental Design, Dean Wurster, Environmental Design Archives, University of California, Berkeley.
15. Gordon Drake to Professor Raymond Jeans, 24 April 1950, Records of the College of Environmental Design, Dean Wurster, Environmental Design Archives, University of California, Berkeley.

The Unit House was planned with five distinct outdoor spaces for expansion of the living areas: a protected terrace roofed over at the end of the living room; a sunny terrace defined with the curved brick seatwall; a shade terrace with a translucent cover supported by a trellis-frame; a sheltered area protected by trees and planting; finally, a future children's play yard visible from the kitchen. Luxury living conditions were achieved at extremely low cost both indoors and in the garden terraces. (Additional pictures on pages 68-71.)

About This Book

In his seven years of professional architectural activity, the late Gordon Drake designed approximately 60 residences, of which less than a fourth were built, one prefabricated unit, two tracts, and six commercial projects which never got beyond the drawing board. He graduated from the University of Southern California, but he never became a registered architect. He died in January, 1952, at the age of 34.

Why, then, a book about Drake and his architecture?

Those of us who were fortunate enough to know him and share both his enthusiasms and his broodings believe that this volume has significance for at least three substantial reasons:

1. As a record of design excellence.
2. As an inspiration to other creative minds.
3. As an exhibit of things of beauty for the delight of any sensitive person.

Though Drake's architectural accomplishments were few in number, each design was of a quality and character that lift it above the status of simply satisfactory performance to the level of distinguished architecture. It is a fact that no architect's work, except for that of the historically renowned or of the few mature "greats" of our own time, has ever been more widely published and applauded both here and in foreign lands than this mere handful of work by a youthful practitioner. There is something here far more important than houses. The ingredients of genius are implicit, if not self-evident. Fine accomplishment in any era, we believe, deserves permanent, public record.

Drake's consuming belief in the importance of architecture; his almost fierce self-criticism; and his constant striving, despite misunderstanding on the part of many who might have helped further the dream, toward that something better; that refinement of detail; the serene integration of plan, structure, and finished design; are all hallmarks of an inspired architectural approach. He was not only determined to create the very best architecture in his power; he was determined that good architecture could and eventually would be extended to everyone. Students of today, the architects of tomorrow, can hardly fail to have their own sights raised with this extraordinary example before them.

Though comparatively few are or will be engaged in the actual creation of architecture, there are thousands who respond to and are nourished by objects of beauty in whatever creative field they are found. For them, this should prove to be a record of rare value.

Hence, the book.

We salute one who was gifted beyond his years; a truly devoted architectural personality; a young man whose talent and determination joined, if only briefly, to produce bright beauty in a moment of world confusion.

George A. Sanderson
Feature Editor
Progressive Architecture

*"the few architects of today who do
wonderful buildings . . . weren't handed these principles
as a gift; they seized them through
work, through struggle and through sacrifice"*

The story of Gordon Drake is the story of American architecture from the late 1930's to 1951. His short and crowded career personalizes the Western architectural revolution which grew out of a new awareness of environment, a depression, a war, and an intense moral struggle.

Gordon Drake was born in Childress, a small town on the plains of Texas, on March 19, 1917, barely three weeks before America's entry into World War I. Before the year was out, his father was serving overseas and his mother had settled in Fresno, California, with her sons Max, the older by ten years, and Gordon.

We see him first at 19 through his mother's eyes—an aimless, easy-going boy with carefree charm. Living now in San Diego, he was a brooding, sensitive dreamer; he saw cloud patterns reflected on the high, sunlit lakes where he swam and fished; he watched the movement and shimmer of eucalyptus leaves and the play of light and shadow in the hills where he wandered; he felt the deep, challenging rhythm of the ocean on which he sailed.

His mother, seeing him stand at times in daydream, noting the occasional discontent, the brooding aimlessness with which he drifted through the spendthrift days of a perpetual summer sun, agreed to send him to Hawaii for a time. His brother, Max, now married and serving as a Navy pilot in the Islands, would care for him and he could study at the University of Hawaii.

We see him again a year later when he first plays the role of "architect." He had just returned from Hawaii. With financial encouragement from Max he built a house for Max and his wife in Coronado.

It was this year—1937—that he enrolled at the University of Southern California in Los Angeles. There he studied under Carl Troedsson of Sweden, first as a student, subsequently as a draftsman. After graduating in architecture he worked as a draftsman with Harwell Hamilton Harris.

He later wrote that from Troedsson he learned that architecture was "a thing of the spirit." Harris gave him insight in building to catch the California he loved and to develop the concept of indoor-outdoor living—all with such a discipline of logic that his influence was later to be confused with the Japanese or Oriental influence.

In 1941 he married, and a few months later he sailed from San Diego, a combat engineer unit officer in the Marine Corps. War was an enforced interlude; first and last, he felt himself an architect. All thought, every experience, each relationship, had to be fitted into this image.

And he did not embrace the idea of an architectural career timidly. At 24, a Marine overseas, he wrote to his mother: "Somehow I feel that one day I shall be a great architect, that because of me—of you—many people shall go from the slums to the green grass, to the shade of the trees, feel the breeze across their bodies, see an untainted blue sky. . . . I feel that I shall have found a moment, that I'll write books, have disciples. The star will flash across the world."

He had ten years to make his star flash.

1 THE ISLANDS:
five years of war

In Gordon Drake two men—an architect and a Marine combat leader—fought on the South Pacific beachheads. One was getting a dirty job done; the other was planning a future. The drives that possessed both were equally intense.

The cheapness of life in war only intensified the dearness of his dream. The creative Drake was now caught in a compelling force; he had no other choice but to express himself through architecture.

To the men around him and to Drake, the word "home" took on many wide-spread meanings. "Home," over and above their personal dreams, was their return to civilian life, their prospects of finding jobs and buying homes in a land of inflation and rising costs.

"Home" to him was a familiar landscape: bright morning light, clear mountain lakes, spiked green pines, sun-dusted chaparral. The details of the California he had grown up in became meaningful to him as he sat in the listless heat of bloody war in the tropics. Part dreamer, part architect, he made sketches of the houses he would build when the war was over—California houses in a California setting that were less a symptom of a fighting man's

Construction of the Haleakala Theatre (above and left) was by a Marine construction group working on a day and night basis to be ready for the scheduled opening day. Drake's only request was to be allowed to do the job without interference and be given all men, tractors, and equipment that he needed. Twenty-one days later the theatre was opened.

homesickness than an architect's growing awareness of the inseparableness of house and environment.

For a would-be architect on an island, "home" and what it meant was something to think about. He and a good friend, Marine Major Louis Soltanoff of an amphibian group, discussed it: the oncoming era in which thousands of veterans would return to the United States with immediate needs of homes and jobs.

The situation formed itself into an opportunity—for the men to turn from the destructive activities of war to the constructive ones of peacetime housing, for Soltanoff and himself as draftsman and architect to supply a particular market demand—and finally it formed into a plan. By the time Soltanoff was assigned to another island, they had decided that after the war they would build houses together. They would use ex-Marine labor, build for returning veterans, and design for a California environment.

Before he sailed for home, Drake had a chance to prove his versatility and his capacity for work. A theatre for servicemen on Maui had been started, but for some reason construction had been interrupted, and Drake was asked to take it over. Appropriately it was his last wartime task.

Instructions were that the building had to be completed in three weeks. Drake's only request was that he be allowed to continue without interference and be given all men, tractors, and bulldozers that he needed. "I took it still-born," he said, "columns and trusses in place and tried my darndest to bring it to life." Twenty-one days later the theatre was opened.

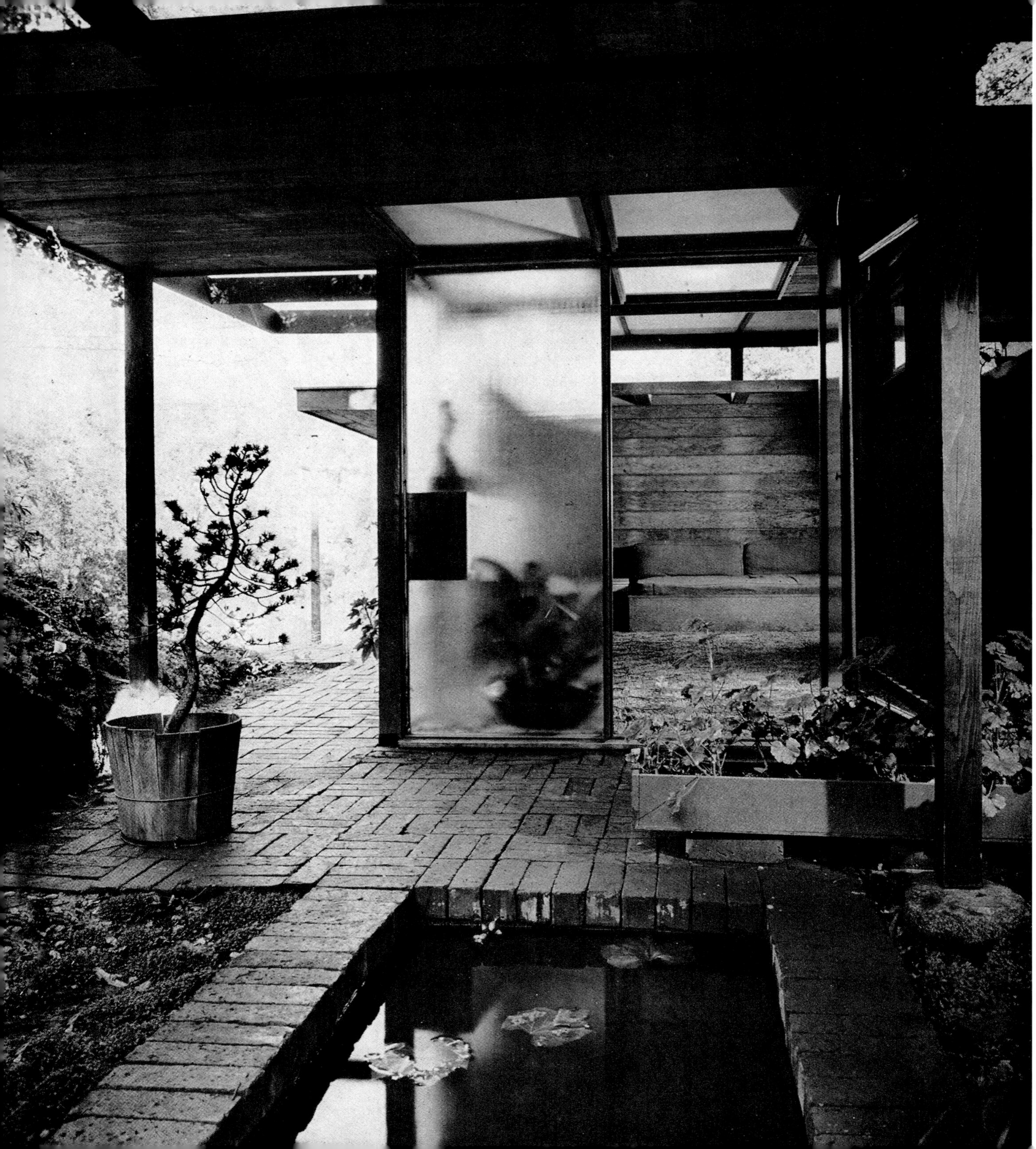

2 LOS ANGELES: the west

Entrance door (left) of Drake's own house in Los Angeles, California, opens on a broad brick terrace and garden pond. A good proportion of the outside area is paved to cut down on the maintenance. This photograph was taken soon after the construction was completed; most of the planting filled in to create a verdant effect with the first year. The house was framed with 4"x 4" posts set 6' on center with redwood plywood used on the exterior and horizontal 1"x 8" shiplap on the interior walls.

In 1946 he was released from the Marines and back on the West Coast. To him, it was his West now—possessed all the more for a five-years' absence. He understood his land and honored it and would now help other people to see it as he did.

He saw the West, first, as a symbol of opportunity, a promise. And the power of a symbol is limitless, both to an architect standing on the threshold of building a postwar world and to the droves of newcomers establishing new homes.

He saw the West through the eyes of the newcomers: as a bright new land, drenched in sunshine and covered with flowers, a place for all-year outdoor living; as a way of life, easy going, informal, neighborly, with a day at the mountains or seashore or desert a matter of whimsy and a few hours' drive.

But he also saw it realistically. He knew it rained in California. He knew how stifling California heat could be. He knew it was sometimes chilly at night. He knew that easy-going neighborliness depended on satisfied, easy-going neighbors. He knew that all the newcomers would not be able to reach out of any window and pluck an orange.

By this time, his strong feeling for environment had formulated into some usable architectural concepts. He believed that a house in California should be everything the West was, actually and symbolically, and that it was the architect's function to provide—through design and materials and engineering principles and words—a complete awareness of both the house and its setting.

He believed that a house and its surroundings should contain a continuing series of emotional experiences—that it should be designed and furnished to be restful and exhilarating, tranquil and exciting, a place of solitude and a place of expansiveness. He believed that it should cover with the inward protection of a cave, and open to the stimulation of the sky.

He believed that a complete house should serve the come-and-go moods and the esthetic, emotional and practical needs of the family within it. As a house builder, with knowledge of exposure, land, climatic conditions, and as an artist, with vision to appreciate and tools to communicate, it was his duty to either provide the orange tree or, in redwood country, help the redwood tree to serve better.

He believed that a house was not only a part of its larger natural environment but also a part of its particular site. He wrote: "We used to think of the 'house' as a building that sits on a piece of 'property.' Now that idea has changed so that certain parts of the house relate closely to the outside (terraces and courts). Well, I want to start with the idea that the property is in reality the outside limit of 'living' and explain the whole idea with symbols that the average person can understand. By that I can arrive by experimentation to certain devices that people who already have houses can use to extend their living."

And he believed that he could, by respecting the outdoors and building to include it, design houses high in livability for a low cost. To provide elaborate, polished luxury for people who could afford to buy luxury was one thing; to provide the experience of luxury for those who would appreciate it was another. "The one thing I do know with certainty," he declared, "is that I intend to use my life to accomplish good, and if I work, build and learn, one day—perhaps in many years—this will be achieved."

He and Soltanoff set to work to put these ideas into effect.

They purchased an inexpensive hillside lot in Los Angeles—a lot that ran straight up and down an embankment of rock foundation. With picks, shovels, and wheelbarrows, their group of veterans carried out the equivalent of three freight cars of dirt and rock. For him, it was as heady as it was backbreaking. In four months the house was completed, at a total cost of $4,500. An additional $300 provided the extra furnishings: chairs, mats, a coffee table, fabrics for covering and curtains.

In 1946, *Progressive Architecture* offered its first annual award of recognition to architects attempting to improve contemporary standards. Gordon

Front door shelter (above) embraces tree and hillside planting to merge the structure with its surroundings. Louvered fence-screen gives a measure of privacy to the living room terrace; obscure textured glass gives impression of unlimited space and relationship to the outdoors.

The brick-paved terrace (above) doubled the the living space of Drake's house and created an illusion of space seldom achieved under minimal conditions. Preserving the native trees and hillside prevented the new garden from seeming raw and unplanted.

Extension of the roof rafters beyond the eaves forms a structural trellis related to the exposed construction inside. This view of Drake's house shows the relation of the terrace, pool and entrance.

Drake entered his house, photographed by Julius Shulman, in the competition.

The architects who came to judge found a compact three-room house mushrooming from a wooded California hillside. The house pockets a small terraced garden, paved and planted sparingly for easy maintenance. A louvered wood screen shields the entry from the rest of the terrace; a rectangular lily pond and a planting box filled with red geraniums dramatize it into courtyard importance.

The basic shell of the house is a 12-by-18-foot room, with the sleeping and living areas at each end separated by a compact kitchen, bathroom, and utility closet. A fabric drapery on tracks provides privacy for the sleeping area; a free standing partition between the kitchen and living area has a structural grille to facilitate serving. A gallery runs along one full side, adjacent to the terrace.

It is a house of space, in spite of its dimensions. Every element leads the eye beyond the actual enclosure. A view is built in with ceiling-line clerestory windows—a view of changing sky, shifting light, and moving tree tops. From the living room, the gallery and the terrace beyond become a part of the

Living room corner of the Mesa house in Carmel (opposite page) features a copper-hooded firepit, a built-in couch and radio-phonograph unit and a chance to see into a small garden terrace through two clear glass doors on the opposite side. (Additional pictures on pages 62-65.)

The west terrace of Drake's house (below) is shaded by the native trees and screened from the road by a louvered screen adjacent to the front door. Bricks were laid on sand and pitched away to drain the water downhill. The site and the construction were truly merged into one living unit.

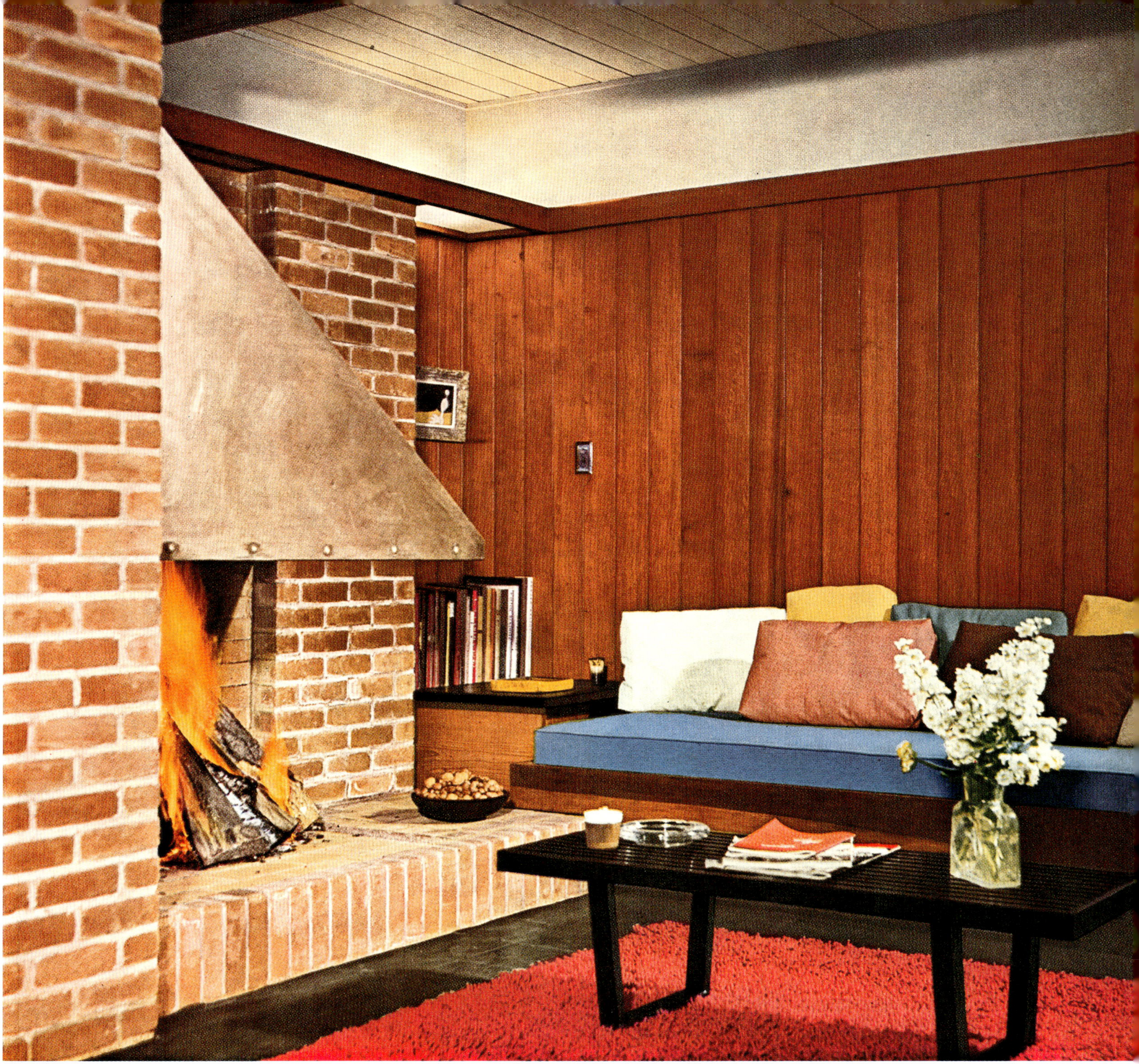

Living room couch and coffee table (right). Room has horizontal shiplap wall finish, ceiling of white celotex material with redwood batt to cover the joints. Emphasis on textures of matting, natural finished wood and glimpses of the hillside beyond gave unusual distinction to Drake's first postwar house.

Sleeping corner (below) is protected with only a fabric drapery; the intention was to give the minimum of privacy and the maximum of the amount of space possible. In later solutions, Drake used sliding shoji panels to solve the problem.

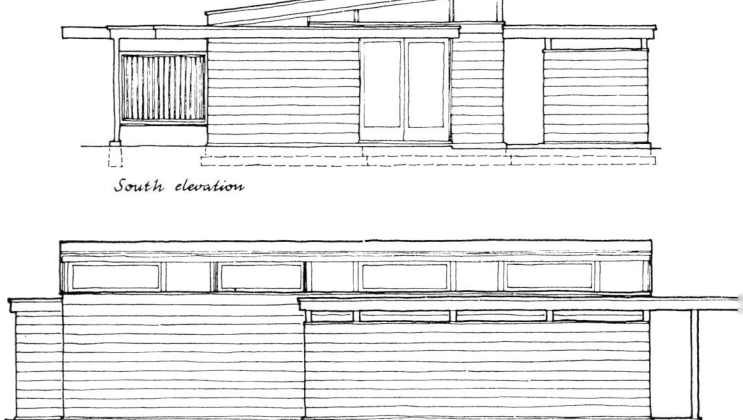

South elevation

East elevation

West elevation

Most of the furniture (above) is in the form of storage shelves and drawer units which are built into the house, thus minimizing the amount of portable furniture that is necessary to furnish the house for economy's sake.

(Above left) looking toward the living area past the built-in dining table; flower arrangements, art forms, architectural color, straw matting, colorful fabrics in upholstery and the pillows—all form an outstanding arrangement of Drake's own elements of gracious living.

View through the front door (left) to garden pool and paved terrace beyond.

indoor decoration. On mild days, the wide glass doors from the gallery to the terrace open to the outdoor living room.

Ducts in the concrete slab foundation keep the house evenly heated. Air, when cooled, returns back to the centrally located heater to be warmed and redistributed.

Interior colors are the natural colors of the building materials and of the land. The Douglas fir walls, stained and waxed to a warm honey-brown smoothness, and the lacquered slate-blue table tops are a muted background for occasional bright touches in furnishings.

Here, then, for $8 a square foot, was the prototype of the minimum house —a house in which the costs were cut without the sacrifice of comfort. It achieved the living amenity of a house many times its size, conjuring up the feeling of airy spaciousness, at peace with and a part of the surrounding landscape.

In the opinion of the judges, the beauty and charm and basic soundness of the house represented a triumph of individual effort. They saw it as a sincere expression of human individuality, an important contribution to society. They termed the plan—so much living in so little space—as brilliant; they cited it for its thoughtful imagination.

Gordon Drake's house was co-winner of the *Progressive Architecture* First Annual Award.

In writing of it, the editors said: "Seldom does one see work in which structure, site, and clients' needs merge so completely in the process of design. Conditioned by the particular circumstances, the construction system here is also the esthetic concept; there is nothing superfluous, nor is the whole in any sense parsimonious. The simple elegance of pencil-thin shadows contrasted with heavy darks under the overhangs results from the knowing use of structural essentials, and helps produce the feeling that this house grows from its site."

Drake's first postwar house was an expression of his individuality. It embodies his love for the outdoors, his recognition of an architect's social obligation, his awareness of light and shadow and movement, his respect for restrained elegance and simplicity.

Designs of the house and analyses of his work were featured in many American magazines, in the French magazine *L'Architecture d'Aujord'hui*, in Sweden's magazine *Form*, and in several other international publications.

At 29, he began to know what it was to see his star flash.

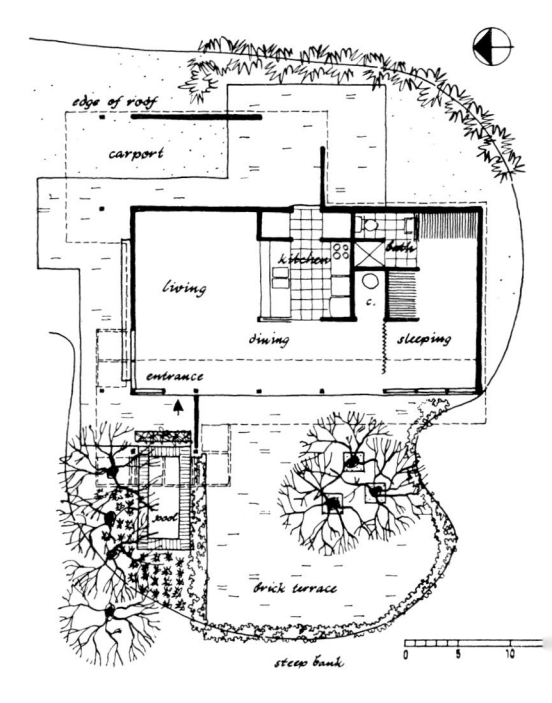

Gordon Drake and Louis Soltanoff took four months to complete the house for the amazing cost of $4,500, which included built-in furniture. For an additional $300 they completed the dwelling with chairs, mats, coffee table, a few fabrics for the bed and curtains plus paintings and sculpture. The plan was compact but spacious in concept and feeling; the structural system was simplified to be built by inexperienced labor; the results were sensational, since this is what many returning GI's hoped to buy.

3 LOS ANGELES: the city

What you gain upon the roundabouts, you lose upon the swings.

The success of his first house was to Gordon Drake the roundabout. He anticipated, then, the swings.

His Marine group gradually disbanded. "The sad truth is that it takes much more than willingness to construct our drawings," he wrote to George A. Sanderson, the Feature Editor of *Progressive Architecture*. He hired two established and experienced contracting firms to take over the construction.

His marriage ended in divorce. There were conflicts in his personal relationships. He was able to throw himself head over heels into a friendship at one moment, stand back and look at it the next.

He was as verbal about and able to be clinically absorbed in the emotional facets of his personal life as he was about his work. His struggle to establish definable relationships applied to his friends, the people with whom he worked, as well as to his surroundings. As an artist, needing first to understand and second to be understood, it was necessary to submit to every emotion—even to seek the emotion—to find the principle.

But to Drake, emotional involvements, like everything else, had to fit the pattern of his work; when they conflicted, he stepped away from them. "Unfortunately, whenever a choice is presented between my work and my personal feelings, a choice isn't really necessary. Happiness or loneliness have absolutely no importance to the work I do."

It was a year of little contracted work but of tremendous output. He could, he claimed, produce enough creative work to keep eight draftsmen busy, but there was not enough contracted work to do it. His work attracted the young, idealistic, and budgeted; he turned away many, advising them to postpone building until costs were lower. For the potential clients who could afford the risks of inflation, he refused to produce fashionable architecture.

"Either I draw too much, or I'm inefficient (on warm spring days I daydream) or I'm a poor slave driver. I refuse to be a businessman. My work is architecture, and I will not let money force me to turn out work that I'm not completely satisfied with."

His architectural writing brought him some reward, his drawing comparatively little. He redefined and crystallized his architectural concepts in magazine articles. In letters he elaborated on his principles and set down the separate but complementary relationship he established between his work and private life.

"I don't know which achieves great buildings," he wrote, "love or ruthlessness. But I do know that they will be achieved. In some ways the war was bad ... the philosophy of achieving the end result and to hell with the means is strong medicine for the fragile artist. I'm very much afraid that in many ways I never left those beaches." He added, as an afterthought, "Ruthless was a poor word. It would be better to say that I will work as I see fit, and according to my conception of right and wrong, regardless of whether or not it concurs with established codes or conceptions. I think any means are justified that result in truth and beauty."

He was teaching at the University of Southern California, living in Los Angeles. The city had been his point-of-return for some fifteen years. Suddenly, in 1947, he felt it bore no relation whatever to the city he had left in 1941. He felt he was walking around on the streets of Rome. He saw it as a city destroying itself and being destroyed by the automobile. He wrote again to Sanderson: "I don't know where the community exists anymore. It stretches from the sea to the Sierra Madres and from the outer rim of the San Fernando valley, 50 miles north, to Long Beach to the south. Pasadena has retained some aspects of a city, but it's like a tired old dowager who wants to doze in the sun. . . . It's the nature of the place that it's impossible to be near anything and have anything but exasperating living conditions. On the other end of the scale is complete withdrawal in a house some 30 miles away that becomes an isolated retreat. Restaurants are scattered. . . .

Preliminary studies (right) for a bachelor's house in Los Angeles completed in the fall of 1951. Entrance to dwelling is at the bedroom-den-balcony level; kitchen and living-dining area are at a lower level. This house represents a gradual change in Drake's thinking and style. The concept of big-scale space and oversized decked area gives great feeling and dimension to a small living unit not achieved before in his design and building. Garage-carport offset to permit access to a difficult street and parking problem. Clipped overhangs are a departure from his usual detailing.

You think nothing of driving 20 miles for supper and then having to wait in line...."

"I burn a candle each night to the gods." He burnt the candle at both ends, working far into the night, carrying fatigue with his absorption. "I've got to go to bed," he wrote at the end of a letter. Then a thought struck him: "Oh, yes!" "...?" "I can't even recall what I was going to say...."

He designed, built, and entered the Spillman house in *House and Garden's* 1947 Architectural Awards competition. It won second prize. He entered the Presley house in the Second Annual *Progressive Architecture* contest, and it won a Mention. In July, 1947, he went to New York to receive, with much acclaim, the award for his first house. He returned to Los Angeles feeling "completely revived, both mentally and physically. Life is a kind and wonderful thing again."

One roundabout down, one swing to balance it; another roundabout was upon him. His reputation grew. His work increased. He bought a car, dressed for success. He took time to relax in his sailboat. He signed the contract for the Malibu house. In one week he picked up $4,400 in fees. His debts were paid, his overhead was relatively small, he had clients waiting for his time.

He was successful, and dissatisfied.

One afternoon he looked up from his drawing board and felt the noises of Wilshire Boulevard pushing hard against the walls of his studio. He pushed back his stool and took off for the Sierra.

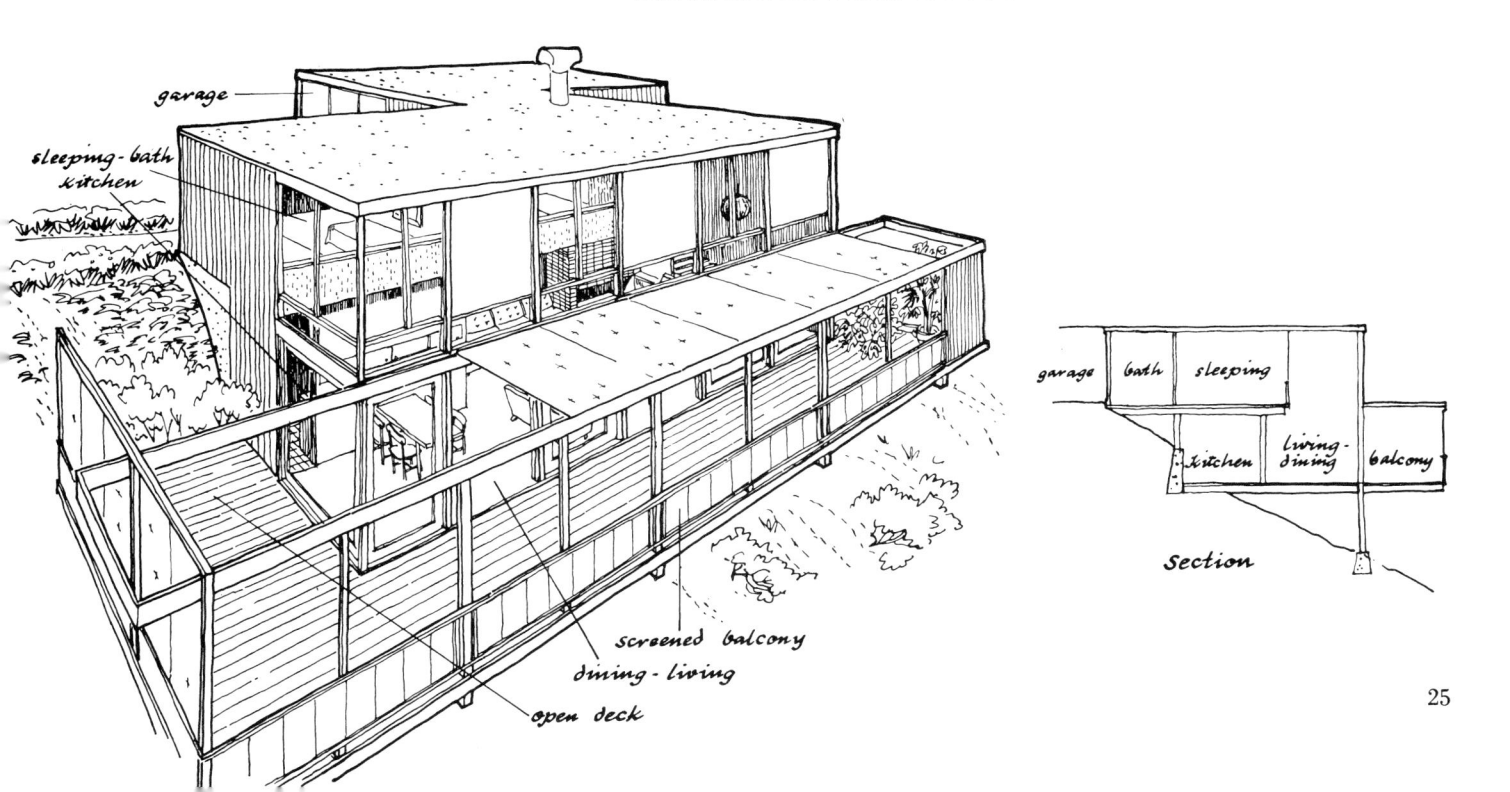

Sketch for a house in the Midwest commissioned by a Michigan architect who wished to expand his professional horizon and thinking with his own house. The crisp draftsmanship of the sketch-studies reflected Drake's thinking along structural forms.

4 THE SIERRA

In the still, brooding remoteness of the high Sierra, above a lake dark with pine shadows, it was a time to analyze—to look with a dissecting eye at what he was, what he was doing, and why he was doing it.

"The architect's purpose must be three-fold. To build. To teach. To propagandize. The buildings can represent his contribution as an individual, but that knowledge that has been gained must be passed on to others in the profession and those training to enter it. If the intellectual breadth has become so frozen that details and development must be kept under lock and key so that others cannot use them in the interest of progress, then that person or office no longer has the right to the name of Architect."

To build. To teach. To propagandize. Over the last year he had done all three. He had built and learned from the Spillman and Presley houses. He had passed on the professional knowledge he had gained to students at the University of Southern California. He had used his writing to define and expand upon architectural concepts to other architects and to the layman.

He was fulfilling adequately the externals of the architect's function. To what purpose? Was it enough for an architect, contributing his ideas in the shape of buildings and words, to contribute to anything as specific as a client or a student or a reader, or anything as general as society?

He must look again to his environment to find a more concrete and meaningful focus. For the *Architectural Forum* in 1947 he wrote:

"The dominant factor in the development of California's domestic architecture has been the existence of a growing native tradition—or, rather, the lack of a stifling formal tradition. The resulting freedom of thought has given the architect an untrammeled concept that does not exist in other parts of the country.

"Geographically, many California cities are located upon land so mountainous that they defy the usual gridiron plan; thus sites have the grace of vista, sun, wind and privacy. Climatically, a season of heavy rains followed by months of hot sun permits a freedom in breaking down the outside wall to a degree not possible elsewhere. Even in the months of intense heat, the constant breeze from the sea affords coolness. Materially, the availability of wood as an inexpensive building material and the appreciation of its beauty and strength has brought about a refinement in structure and detailing that's almost Oriental in its sparing simplicity. Finally, the concentration of wealth —wealth available for immediate use—has been of great importance.

"Initially, land development took place in the flat valleys that lie between the foothills, a development based upon ease and economy of construction. Today, new residential building is forced to the surrounding hills or to satellite cities miles away. Site considerations, then, are most interesting. From almost any height, a view is given of a sprawling city—particularly magnificent at night—the ranges of mountains, or the sea to the West.

"Assuming the basic needs of the client, the plan is freed and yet limited by the climate. Portions of the house may be directed to the breathtaking views, but there also must be the completely sheltered garden that becomes part of the living area, and finally the protected shelter where one may withdraw completely from the outside. Other considerations that affect the form of the roof and the disposition of wall and mass are the extremes reached by both sun and rain in their major seasons.

"Perhaps the use of light itself is the greatest influence on planning. The quality of light of each part of the day must be used or limited as the use of the particular living area requires. This is accomplished by clerestory venting windows, sheltering walls of the sleeping rooms, translucent screens that turn sun into coolness, and glass walls that allow the full measure of sunlight to play in the general living spaces.

Sketch for a mountain cabin (above) produced for Sunset Magazine July 1950 issue. Structure would serve equally well for summer or winter use. Second-story entrance through ski work room for heavy snow conditions with access by a ramped stair. Trellis and screen wall provide an ample outdoor garden terrace during the snow-free months for sunning and entertaining. Construction to be of rough-sawn materials and native rocks. "Teepee" roof would be strong enough to take any snow load. On the facing page is the cutaway end view.

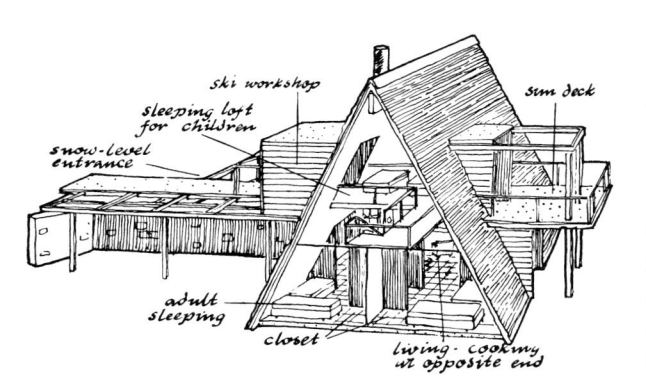

"Green planting to relieve the harsh dryness of the summer months is used to interpenetrate the living space and thus relate the garden to the house. Conversely, by the use of an overhead screened trellis that is a continuation of the roof plane, the actual living area flows out and embraces the garden.

"For the first time, natural wood is enjoying greater use in contemporary work than plaster, for economy nods toward the use of wood as an exterior wall covering. Rough-sawn boards on exterior walls for form and texture may be used as a foil for the magnificent sophistication of waxed plywood on the interior.

"Youth has learned to recognize that contemporary architecture represents a way of living that transforms the home from its role as mere shelter to the center of an existence. Architects capable of making this possible must work toward this end as one phase of their practice. This, of course, can be economically possible only when it is approached through industrialized mass production, or when the field of speculative building is entered with the force of outstanding design. The time has now come when decent living no longer should be the exclusive right of the wealthy or the intellectual, but rather must be shared with the great mass of America that cannot afford the luxury of an architect. Realizing the social needs of his time, the architect must accept the responsibility of leadership in this field, regardless of a minimum schedule of fees or any other consideration which has heretofore acted as a moral barrier."

By looking at his California environment through the houses and the people within it, he worked himself back to the challenge of his youth-seen star. But six years later, the distance between the "slums" and the "green grass" was less breathtaking, less dramatic, more specifically bridgeable.

He wrote a friend: "I suddenly found out what the indefinable thing is that I'm seeking in these buildings, and the one thing that has not yet been achieved. I've got to find out what humbleness—or perhaps you can call it humility—is in both myself and my building. . . . Humbleness is not something you can consciously add to the sum total, unless you can find that quality within yourself. At least I can't. For a time there was a tendency—with complete logic and unknowingly—to build monuments to myself. . . . It's difficult to come to this realization, for humility is a quality that I've known very little. But that realization assures the future. . . . I think the best critic of architecture would be a small child. Buildings are judged by whether or not the people who live in them are happy or unhappy."

A star flashing too high and too brightly was as unsatisfying as its admiration. A star need be no less bright for being brought down closer.

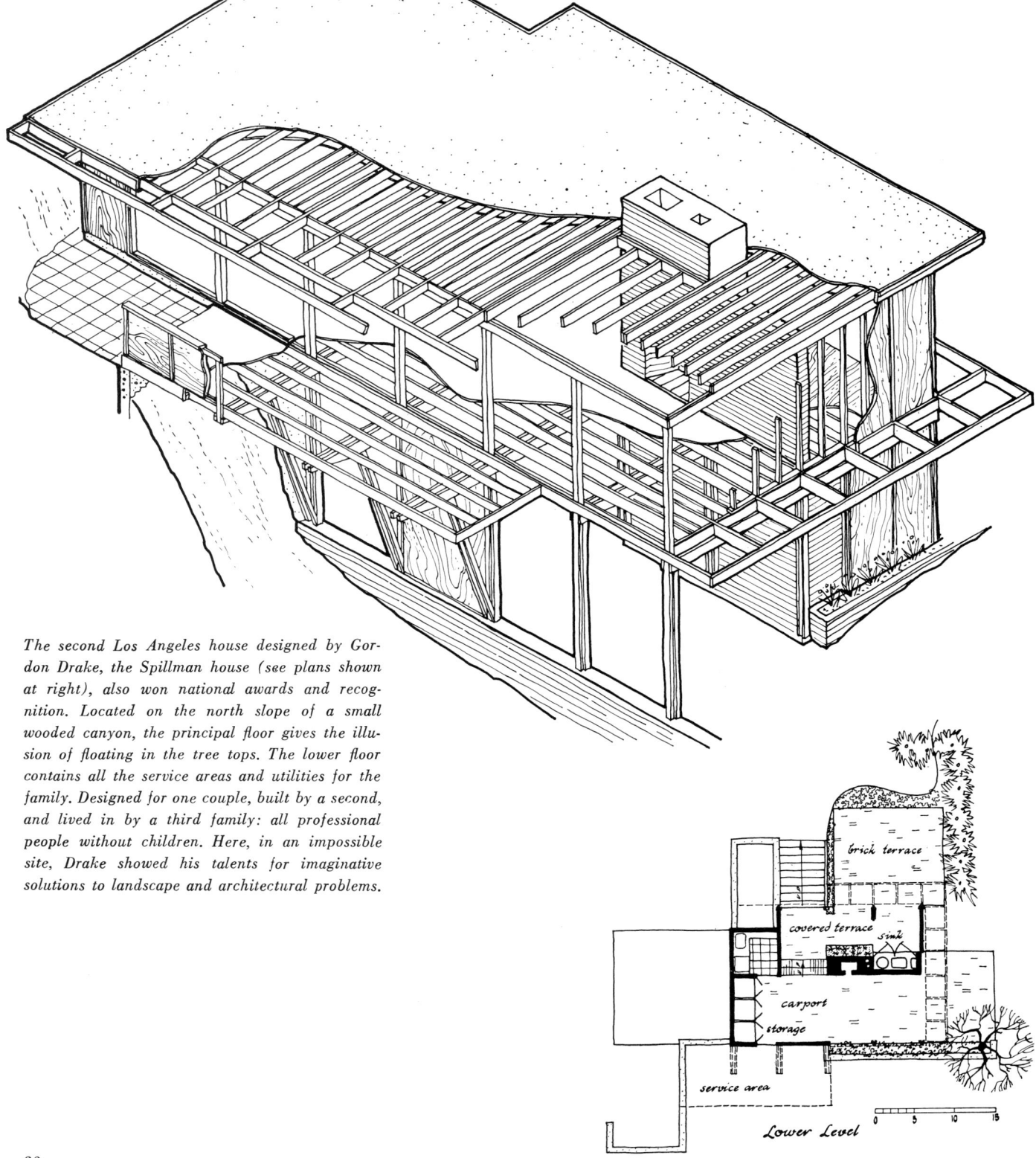

The second Los Angeles house designed by Gordon Drake, the Spillman house (see plans shown at right), also won national awards and recognition. Located on the north slope of a small wooded canyon, the principal floor gives the illusion of floating in the tree tops. The lower floor contains all the service areas and utilities for the family. Designed for one couple, built by a second, and lived in by a third family: all professional people without children. Here, in an impossible site, Drake showed his talents for imaginative solutions to landscape and architectural problems.

Lower Level

5 LOS ANGELES: the houses

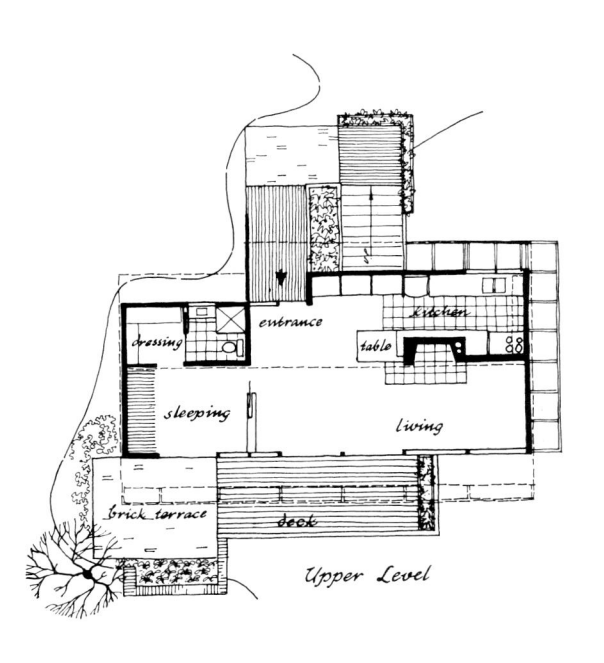

The Spillman and the Presley houses embodied the principles Drake set down in *Architectural Forum*.

The Spillman house, which won second prize in *House and Garden*'s 1947 Award in Architecture (Richard Neutra won the first award), was designed to meet a young couple's individual need. Like his other houses of this period, it was built on an inexpensive and difficult site—a pocket of thickly wooded land cornered by rock cliffs on the north side of a precipitous road.

He used the original isometric drawing to convince the local building inspector that the structure would actually stand up. To avoid a dark ground floor, and because the buildable area was just 30 by 35 feet, the house of fir, plywood, hardboard and brick was raised high into the treetops for sun, view and privacy.

The plan, frankly money-saving, concentrated on essentials, making a virtue of its economies. Living space was extended by a balcony that had the sky for its roof. Below, tucked into the curve of the hill at base level and sheltered from the road by a screen planting and the house itself, was an outdoor sitting room.

The east wall of the Spillman house (above and on next page) is a series of full glazed doors opening to a balcony, which in turn lead to a protected garden terrace set into the hillside. Drake led the way in experimentation with exterior grade plywood panels. Ceiling treatments are invariably rich in interest and color with lighting panels instead of conventional light sources.

View from the interior looking toward the wooded slope; the open construction is unusual even for California living conditions. Here is a direction for the construction of beach or mountain cabins in all sections of the country with the introduction of double glazed window and door units. Construction costs of the Spillman house were in the neighborhood of $7000 in this early postwar period.

This view shows the feeling of a house growing from the site; conditioned by the difficult circumstances, the construction system is also an esthetic concept. The richness of the shade and shadow, the application of color, and the blending of the native plantings are all brought together into a harmonious relationship.

Entry from the carport (right) is up a broad flight of wooden treads protected by a vertical screen. Open areas are used to create a lower garden terrace paved with bricks for low maintenance and easy installation.

Wooden ramp (below right) bridges the space from building to house entrance area. Existing trees were invariably a part of Drake's design; preservation of the growth gave his structures a feeling of maturity seldom achieved on the usual "builder's lot."

Ribbed glass (below) provides privacy to the entrance but admits enough light and shadow to prevent the area from becoming uninteresting. Lighting soffits overhead repeat the pattern of light and shadow during the nighttime. Extensive use of interior planting gives these small houses a continuing relationship with the outdoors.

Careful attention to the site details became an important part of the house for the Spillmans (above): terraces, plant containers, small pools, furniture storage units, tree forms and shadows, screens and fences—all help to expand and enrich the enclosed spaces within the house.

Kitchen alcove (right) is separated physically from the living room by the brick chimney form, yet the food preparation is not visible from the living areas. Built-in table seats four under normal conditions but is large enough for seven under party conditions. The flow of space makes a minimum house seem spacious.

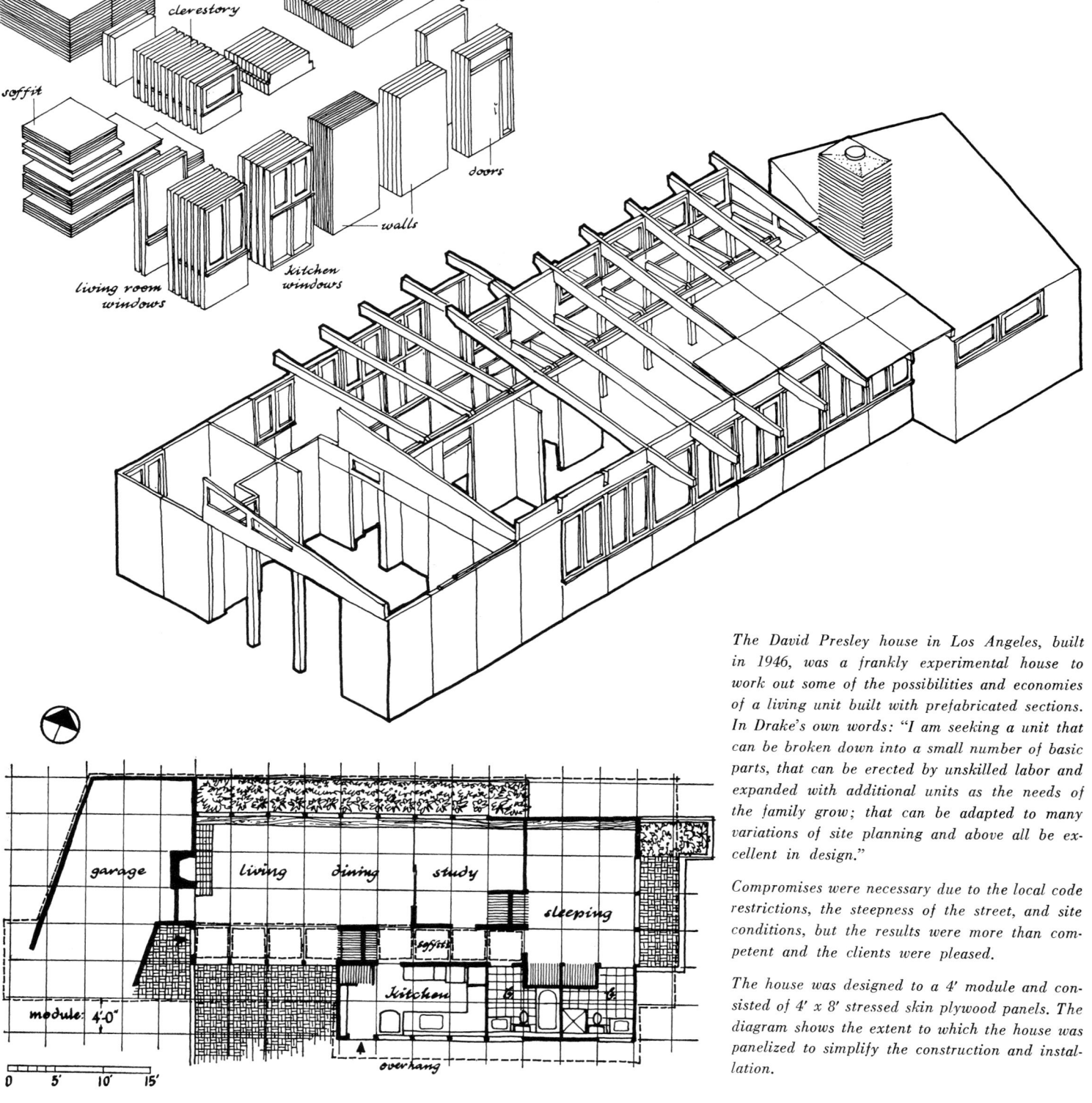

The David Presley house in Los Angeles, built in 1946, was a frankly experimental house to work out some of the possibilities and economies of a living unit built with prefabricated sections. In Drake's own words: "I am seeking a unit that can be broken down into a small number of basic parts, that can be erected by unskilled labor and expanded with additional units as the needs of the family grow; that can be adapted to many variations of site planning and above all be excellent in design."

Compromises were necessary due to the local code restrictions, the steepness of the street, and site conditions, but the results were more than competent and the clients were pleased.

The house was designed to a 4' module and consisted of 4' x 8' stressed skin plywood panels. The diagram shows the extent to which the house was panelized to simplify the construction and installation.

Situated on one of the steepest streets in Los Angeles, the Presley house turns its back on the slope and opens up to the dramatic view of the city. The garage at the left is angled to permit automobile access to the street. Wood screen of grapestakes protects a small garden court which adjoins the entrance hall and living area. Variations in the garden terraces and fences would give many additional opportunities for individuality in mass-produced structures.

Inconspicuous built-in furniture, lightweight partitions, generous expanses of glass, and variations in ceiling height brought the luxury of light and space to the 15-by-39-foot main floor, which included the balcony extension.

The Presley house was more ambitious and more costly—more ambitious because it was an experiment in panel construction, more costly because it was built for a young couple who could afford certain additional features (a custom radio-phonograph combination, many cabinets, a second bathroom, an automatic laundry, etc.)

Here, Drake applied the theories of Greek modular construction—using a basic measure in component parts of the building for eliminating waste and for producing pleasing, rhythmic relationships—to modern housing. He was seeking a unit that could be broken into a number of basic parts, erected by unskilled labor, producing a modular panelized building for low-cost mass product.

The Presley site, high on a hillside, commanded magnificent views: toward the west, the panorama of the city, the near hills of the Silver Lake area, and the succeeding ranges of the Santa Monica mountains beyond; toward the north, the city sprawling at the foot of the sheer wall of the Sierra Madres.

The quality of light was a great influence on Drake's planning: "This can be achieved by clerestory venting windows (shown here above), glass walls that allow full measure of sunlight, or translucent screens that turn the sun into coolness."

Interior and exterior photographs (right, above and below) of the bank of windows facing the city and the view to the north. Built-in cabinets extend the full length of the house to provide all the requirements for storage.

(Above) the living area and the adjoining study in the David Presley house are separated by translucent panels, half-open here. A slot was made in the wall cabinet under windows to allow complete closing of the screens. An occasional guest could be accommodated for short periods by converting the study couch into a bed.

Careful attention was given to detailing of cabinets and screens (above right). Drake had hoped to achieve most of this quality in low-cost houses by the prefabrication of the units on a factory basis; this house was built to demonstrate the possibilities to the HomeOla Corporation.

He composed the house of two rectangular units, the larger for the living areas, the smaller for the service units. The living room and study looked out upon the city below; the master bedroom opened to its own private garden with a natural stand of Scotch broom. The service units, looking directly into the hill, occupied the least desirable portion of the level area.

In the living area, at the heart of the rectangle, he developed a seating group about the fireplace, with the built-in radio-phonograph combination and record and book storage close by. One part of the room is furnished as dining space; sliding screens, which can be lifted off the track and removed, form a disappearing wall to the study.

Bedrooms are at the other end of the rectangle. Storage units divide the bedrooms from the baths. A hall with a ceiling of frosted glass connects the service units and the bedrooms. A built-in dish cabinet stands at the end of this hall,

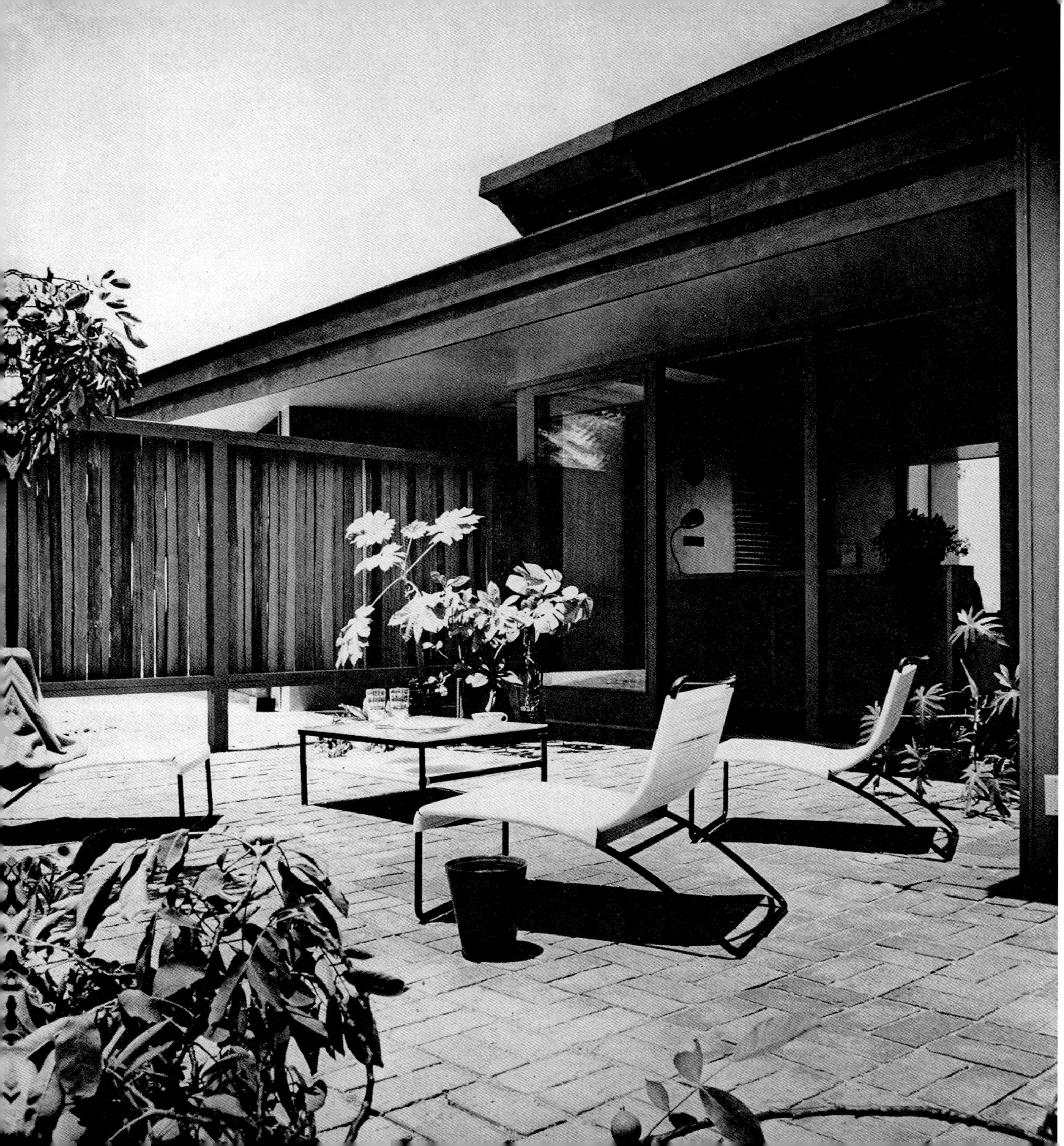

The Presley living room terrace (left) is connected by sliding doors to the main house area. Kitchen service door provides opportunity to serve food and drinks to the outdoor area. Floating fence-screen prevented garden construction from becoming too rustic and heavy in contrast to the trim architectural lines of the house.

providing convenient service to either the dining space or the terrace. A structural trellis defines the circulation portions of the house and carries direct and indirect lighting systems.

He used the natural textures and body of his building materials as color, tone against tone, plane against plane. He chose drapery and upholstery fabrics in reddish browns, sands, terra cottas, and grayed blue-greens to absorb and soften California's sunshine.

View through the bedroom (below) to portion of private garden sun terrace protected from the wind and casual visitors. The east exposure is ideal for a cheerful morning awakening with the early rays of the sun on the floor. Built-in cabinets and mirrored dressing table line the bed wall.

Looking in (below) from the brick terrace which is perched on a ledge overlooking the native hillside growths and the distant cityscape beyond. Wide roof overhang gives partial protection to the glass area. Glass panel slides on a metal track; small overhead windows give ventilation.

In external form, the horizontal lines of the heavy lower roof line relate the house to the ground. Above, the clerestory windows—a delicate tracery—distribute light and ventilation to the inner rooms.

As an experiment, the house was not a total success. The site called for a much freer treatment than the somewhat rigid limits of a structural module. A difficult site at best, it required filling to make it suitable for the slab foundation. The cost of the house was far more than for a conventionally built house: materials for this technique were not readily available, and considering it as a construction pattern to test the feasibility of mass production made it necessary to painstakingly hand-make many parts of it.

But as a house to be lived in—were its people happy? David Presley said: "The lightness and the airiness of the house are actually what we appreciate the most." After living in it, there was no feature they would do without, nothing they would change. The house cost far more than the preliminary estimates, but it was a house that lived with light, sheltered with privacy, captured a fresh breeze. It was a home, the Presleys felt, that could hardly depreciate, either in commercial or intrinsic value.

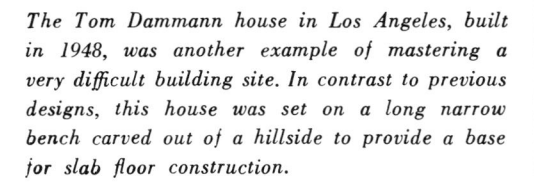

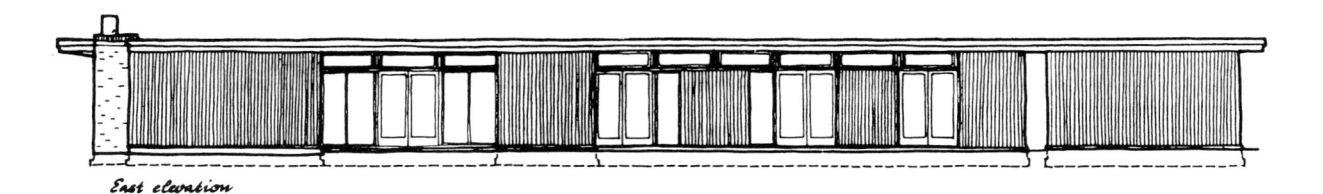

The Tom Dammann house in Los Angeles, built in 1948, was another example of mastering a very difficult building site. In contrast to previous designs, this house was set on a long narrow bench carved out of a hillside to provide a base for slab floor construction.

East elevation

South elevation

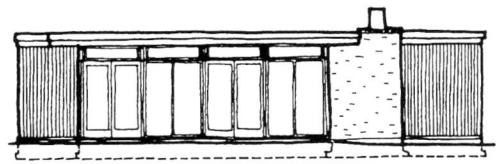

View through the loggia southeast to the living room-study area across the inner garden court. Bringing the outdoor space into the interior may become an architectural cliché in time but it will always give a small house a feeling of luxury. Drake invariably used brick on sand for the terrace paving, since it cost only sixty cents a square foot. The color is related to the interior and the maintenance is low.

Mother's view from the kitchen to the children playing on the paved garden terrace (left). Direct access provides easy service for outdoor dining; high kitchen counter sandwich bar in the foreground, inside the Dammann house, screens lower work surfaces.

Looking down the long corridor (below left) to the bedroom areas and showing, again, the relation of the house to the garden areas. It is possible to enclose the inner court with insect screening to create a lanai.

(Below) sandwich bar for the children's quick lunch; a serving counter for smorgasbord entertaining; a handy place for guest to leave the dirty dishes without running into the kitchen helpers; a good place for casual coffee and conversation.

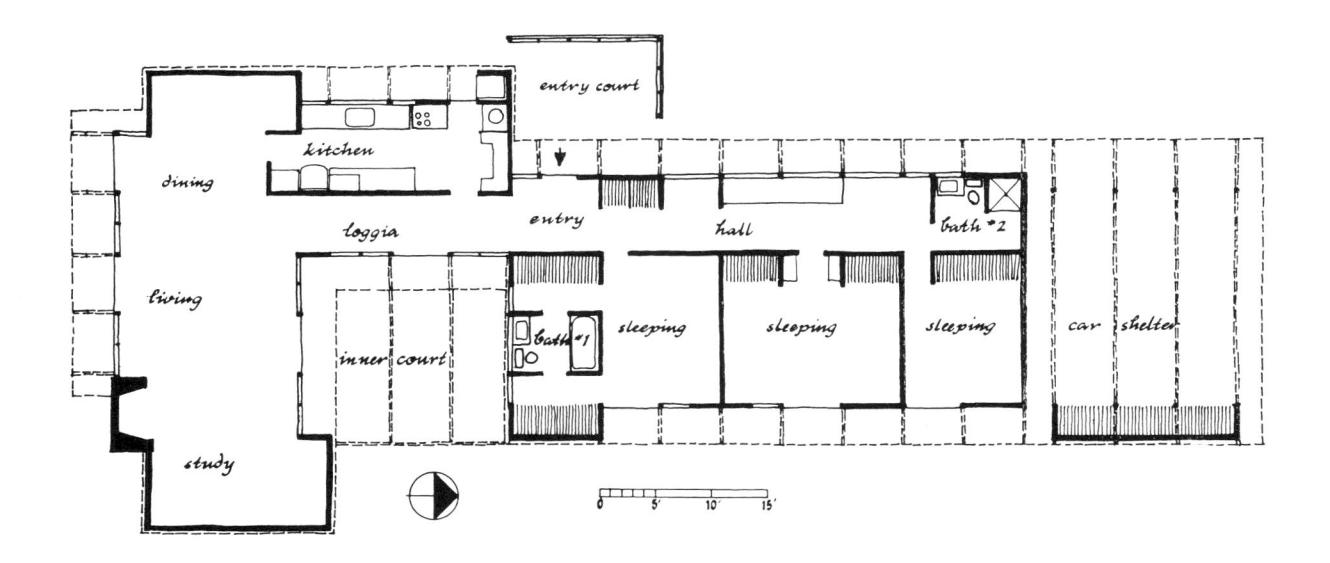

View (below) north to bedroom terraces; each room has a double door swinging to the outdoors. Pleasant views from these rooms are possible by placing the beds to face the east morning light. Continuity of paving around the house gives additional feeling of space.

South side of living room facing directly into the main view (below). Notice the unusual dining alcove solution (see plan), solving the lack of a separate dining room in houses with limited space. See how the dish storage was handled convenient to both kitchen and dining area.

6 CARMEL: the big dream

There are many ways of measuring time—dividing off a man's life by dates. To Drake, a year was time enough to win a war or set the world on fire; to most of the people he talked with, a year was a period of waiting to see what might happen.

January 15, 1948, is a significant date in Drake's story. He sat down that night, late as usual, to write an architect about his new plan—a professional school in conjunction with an architectural office in a small Pacific coast community. "It's just a dream now, but wouldn't that be wonderful? Perhaps it's an odd streak in me. . . . In the last few months the clients have been beating at the door, and I know I could really clean up financially if I opened a drafting factory. It means a hell of a lot to me to shake my head and go up to Monterey and work with a pick and shovel on something that can mean a great deal to many people. . . ."

He had returned from the Sierra feeling done with Los Angeles. Back firmly on the star-route, neither the pencil and paper negotiations for mass production of the modular panels from the Presley house experiment nor the initial plans for the Malibu house could ground him. "The highest form of architecture is one that changes the environment toward a better condition. A house, an apartment, a block, a city, or a region. . . . The only true way you can find the path is to build, and then if it's wrong, attack the particular problem from another direction.

"I must go to Carmel and build a professional building that expresses what I believe in. This must be built with my own hands as an expression of faith. I'm not being mystical. . . . I know only too well how difficult it is to establish a practice and then just when the work comes, walk out and start all over again. . . . Perhaps it means several lean years. That's all quite unimportant, for in ten years one will be able to see the change that has taken place. . . ."

The reference in his letters to the Monterey peninsula and Carmel stemmed from his lecture series at U.S.C. There he acquired a deep sympathy and responsibility toward the architectural students. He understood their eagerness and sensed the disillusionment that would catch so many after they left school.

In the course of his lecturing, Drake made friends with John Boylin, chief of the Industrial Design Department of U.S.C., and William Stutz, an expert in the field of graphic arts and a visiting lecturer.

In the atmosphere of a graduate school, joining with men anxious to join in any search that would lead to a better world, the Big Dream took shape.

This dream would do many things:

It would create complete design centers, bringing together the workings of the architect, the planner, the landscape architect, the designer, to serve every design need of the community—city parks, subdivisions, recreation areas, schools, shopping centers, home remodeling, garden rooms, gardens, factories, containers, labels, furniture, machines.

At its Carmel headquarters it would be a research center, supported through industrial interest tests and experiments in new materials, new methods, and distributing its knowledge through public lectures, exhibitions, publication in consumer magazines and possibly a magazine of its own.

It would build a school that would do for the young graduate architect what an internship does for the graduate doctor. There would be no master-architect teaching his disciples his ideas; it would, rather, be the transition ground between school and practice, preparing the architect—through actual experience in every phase of construction, design, planning, and even in presentation and selling of ideas—to take his place in his community.

A dream begins with broad principles. Drake wrote: "Through research arrive at honest planning. Build. Evaluate. Give these ideas and developments to the community as they desire them. Create that desire."

The center would sell itself to the community in which it located. Ways would be found to make the need for designers, planners, researchers, and teachers understood by everyone in the community. Architecture would not be a luxury enjoyed by 5% of the people; through an architectural center that accumulated, utilized, and spread its knowledge, good design, solid planning, and expert and creative thinking could become as universally available as hammers and nails.

The school would spread its reputation over its graduates wherever they located. Specialized service, consultations, would be available directly from the school or, in other localities, from the top men in the profession who associated with it. No longer would the young architect be forced to build, from a cold start, a reputation in big cities. As a graduate of this school he could go anywhere with the confidence and the seal of practical, top-flight training. Well-known specialists, the backing of big industries, local civic pride, would attract public support and bring national recognition.

Recognition. Drake knew the real meaning of the word—and all its limitations. In two years he had been showered with more publicity than accrues to most architects in a lifetime. In the frantic groping of postwar architecture, he seemed to hold the brightest, cleanest light. There was something in his work that attracted the tired eyes of editors. Publicity did not need to end with satisfying the ego; publicity, he felt, was a force that he could now use to the benefit of himself or anyone of his choosing.

In him, there was the precociousness of the bright boy who had received early fame; there was also the star-gazing bravura of the man not yet 30, not yet legally an architect (he had not taken his state architectural examinations) talking blithely about establishing a nationally recognized, nationally admired professional school. But there was also a Big Man with a Big Dream about a Big Community—and for this, recognition and publicity meant disciples and believers. His own enthusiasm made his Big Dream seem like plausibility with a touch of glory.

He wrote: "Where does the creative act stop and the dictatorial drive take over? You see, one of the problems that I face (and I must conquer) is that throughout the few years when I went from adolescence to maturity I was faced constantly with the problem of evaluating the problem, deciding an immediate course of action, and then throwing so much force behind it that no matter if the basic decision was wrong, the force made it right (the premise upon which the success of the Marine Corps was based).... Now the evaluating process must be slow and soul-searching. It's difficult to throw out action and impatience of resolution and determination, but I'm learning."

Scale model built by Drake to study the first unit of his dream for a studio and training school in the Carmel-Point Lobos area. Since it was to be built by unskilled labor and apprentice designers, the construction was kept to the simplest detail and rough materials.

The dream became specific. The community of Carmel would give support to such a project—several civic leaders consulted were very enthusiastic. Industries would be interested in tests and experiments.

One sizable land development, building and selling fifty houses a year, would bring enough commissions to finance the beginnings. The bank agreed to a loan on one building; the remainder of the financial backing would depend on the work produced.

It was enough. In the fall of 1948 Drake wrote to a friend: "I'm enclosing the first spadeful of earth from the foundations of the office. Finally, I have actually started construction."

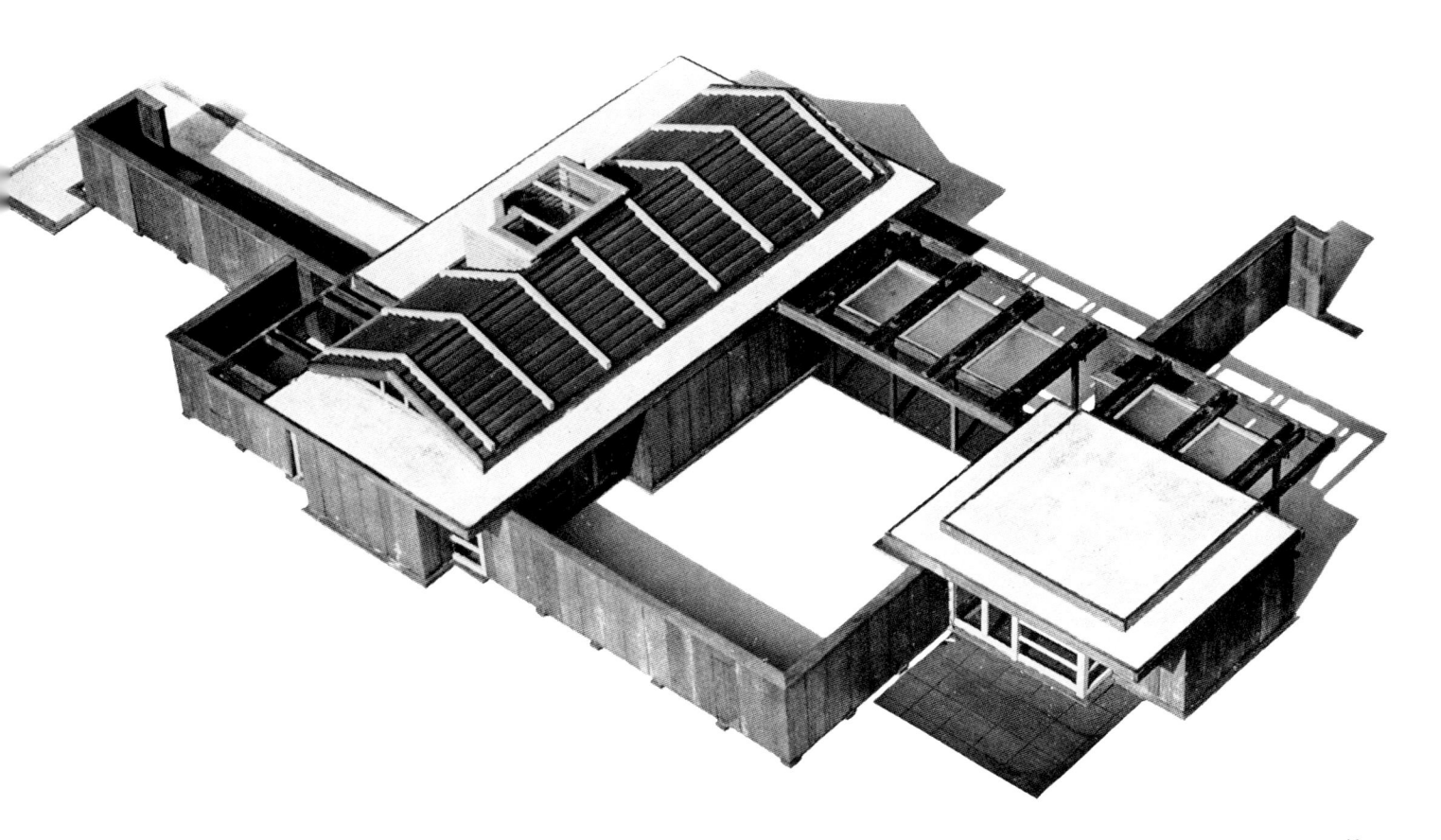

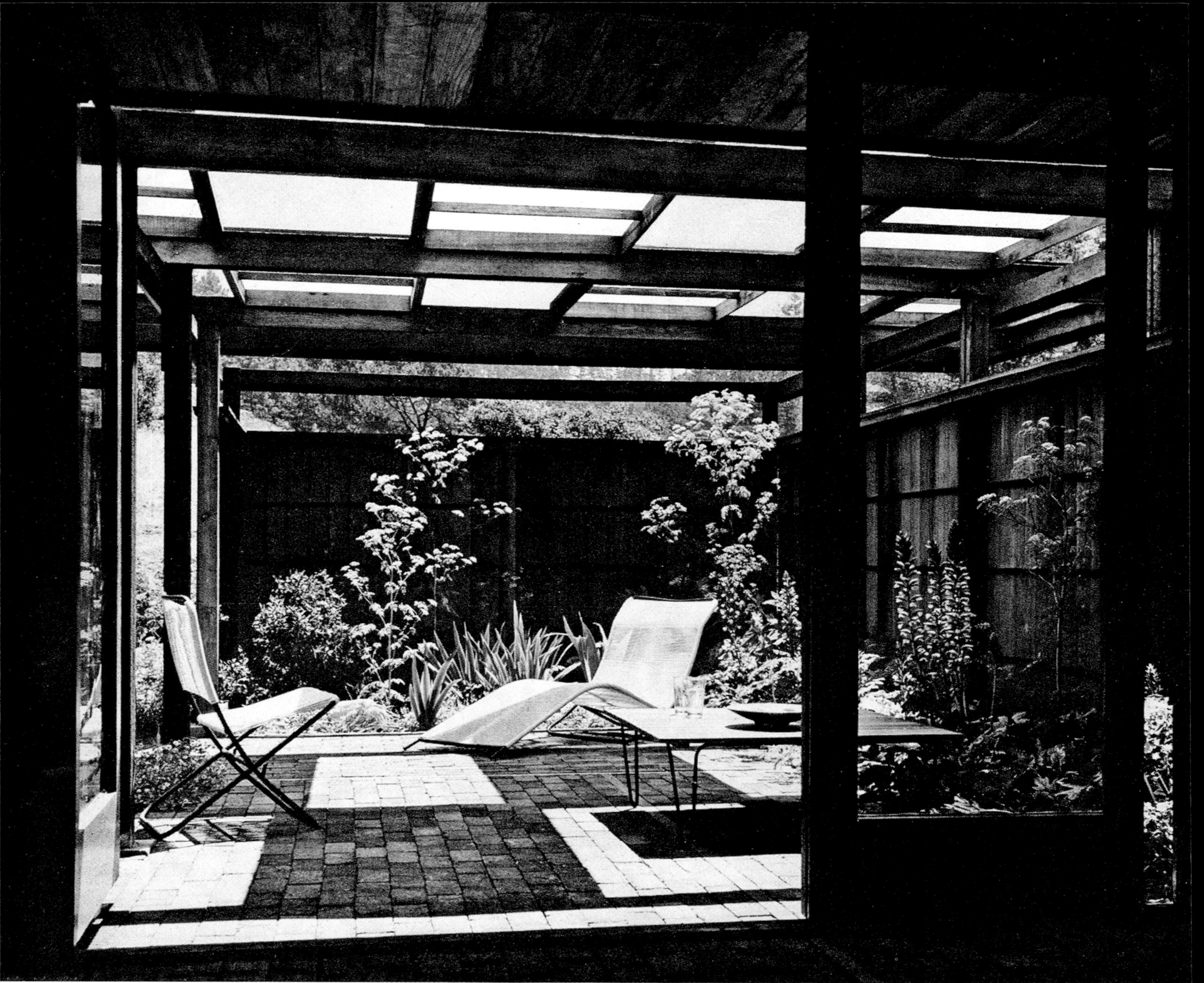

7 CARMEL: the cold facts

The Carmel dream was partially realized but only by Drake's spending his own money and finally nailing the boards and laying the bricks by himself. Overhead movable screens of colored canvas set in frames formed a good solution to the sun problems. Enclosing fence gave the feeling of privacy to the office and windbreak for the terrace. One of the first garden collaborations with Douglas Baylis, the plantings were selected from natives indigenous to the Carmel area to create gardens of low-cost maintenance. Garden furniture designed by Walter Lamb of San Francisco. (Additional pictures on pages 58-61.)

Unfortunately, the dream did not progress according to plan. The Carmel project never got off the ground.

William Stutz suffered a heart attack. The Boylin family, after building a house in Carmel, couldn't wait for the developments of an uncertain future. The Carmel land developers—for whom he designed five houses, with future houses contingent upon their sale—didn't sell houses as fast as they had hoped.

Drake, without income to count on or the company of his fellow-believers to thrive on, decided to bull ahead and at least build the office, spending his own money to do it.

Here again he found compensations. "I guess most of the measure of the good life lies within walking distance," he wrote to George Sanderson. The office site was on a small plateau lying a little above the valley floor, between the mountains and the sea. His acre was on the sun's path; a sheer canyon wall rose above it, a carpet of dark-massed Monterey pines lay below it.

His rented room in Carmel was two blocks from the beach. There was low, obscuring morning fog; there was the sound of the deer in the underbrush; there was the rhythm of the waves; there were long, white-bleached stretches of isolated beach; there was always one more crest of one more hill with the mystery of what was just beyond.

At first he enjoyed his isolation. He was building with his own hands. "I suppose the best thing is to live each day for what it is.... With that, I shall go out and notch some more sills this afternoon." It was a peaceful, simple life, with the added satisfaction of being a gesture against what he thought were the traps and the trappings of city success.

On New Year's Day of 1949 he made a "pilgrimage" to Point Lobos. That night he wrote, "Perhaps this will be the year we have looked forward to for so very long.... I do know that when I am dead, if I do have a ghost, I'm going to be a wisp of fog in the pine trees along the cliffs of Lobos. I'll be a very happy and gentle ghost, too...."

By March, the first house for the land developers was completed. By mid-June, the studio-office was ready. He moved in, waited for clients; he would study for the State board architectural examinations until they came.

He called the first house the Vacation House. It was a week-end retreat, a change of pace, for living easily, entertaining casually, designed to weather with the land. In plan, the house is essentially three rectangles—the sun deck, the main living areas, and the kitchen-bath unit—stepped diagonally one above the other into the contours of the hill behind it and exposing a footing of piers and posts.

Drake wrote his own description: "To enter the house, one walks under a covered arbor set free from the house in the central portion so that one does not have the feeling of being enclosed to a great degree; yet there is enough sense of enclosure and protection that a change of pace is gradually accomplished as one walks from the motor yard, up the steps and into the terrace garden.

"The main entrance is at the end of the arbor. A screen fence makes a baffle into the service yard door to the house; a pane of obscure glass is to the right of the entry, affording a balance of light with the great bank of glass windows on the view side of the living room, and giving one a feeling of anticipation while waiting for the door to be opened. When this door is opened, you see directly ahead the view from the entire east wall of the living room; to the left is the secluded fireplace corner with its bookcases, couch and cabinets; and to the right is a pair of decorative sliding screens which divide the living room from the dining area.

"The screens were designed so that when they are opened or closed in varying degrees, the quality of light coming through the various combinations of frame and fabrics gives the rooms a constantly changing appearance. They

Vacation House in Carmel, California, was built in 1949 as a speculative venture to test the market for week-end retreats in a resort area. Designed so that people can live easily and entertain casually, it will weather gracefully without maintenance problems. The house is basically three rectangles: the sun deck, the main living area, and the kitchen-bath unit. The three units were stepped diagonally one above the other into the contours of the hill behind it, exposing the footings and the piers and the structural system.

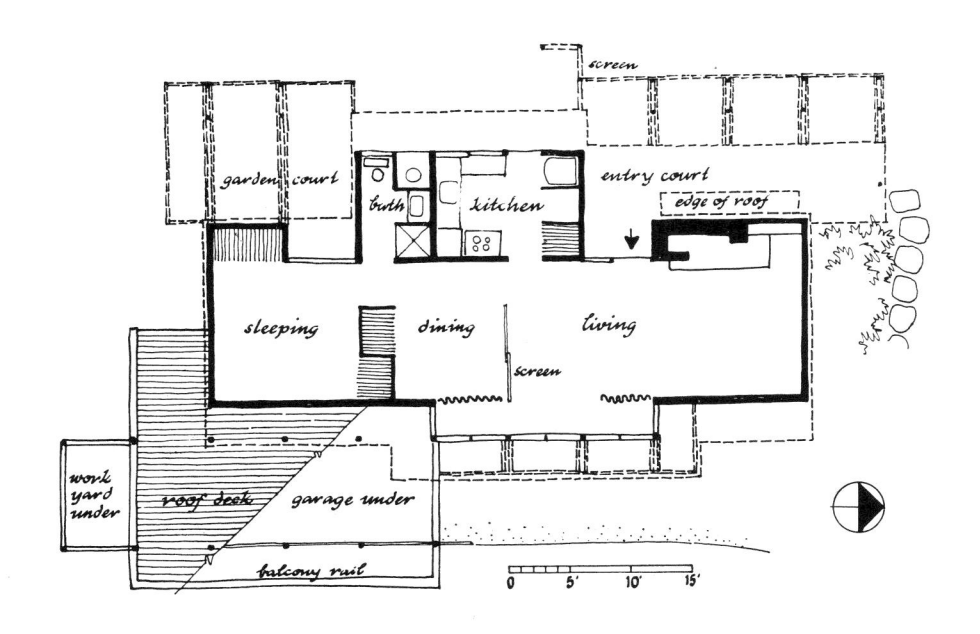

garden court | bath | kitchen | entry court | edge of roof

sleeping | dining | living | screen

work yard under | roof deck | garage under
balcony rail

0 5' 10' 15'

(Above) approach and shelter to the Vacation House: garden trellis support for the protective canopy leading to the front door. Redwood rounds cut six inches thick for paving blocks.

Entrance to Vacation House (left), showing the woodsy effects of planting, paving, resawn redwood siding, shadow patterns of plant forms, textures of floor covering and draperies combined into a harmonious composition.

View (below) from hill above to show sundeck, garden terrace, and entrance relationship. The placement of the house above the access road gives a great feeling of privacy and setback.

Interior view (above) showing glass treatment along the north side; interior arrangements by Frances Baer in collaboration with the designer and photographer.

Detail photograph (right) of sliding panels separating the living room from the dining area. Various materials and textures give richness to a functional device. The screen is modeled on the idea of the Japanese shoji panel but made practical by materials that resist dust and abuse common to week-end and vacation homes. Overhead sliding track, attached to structural member, was used to keep the floor covering unbroken.

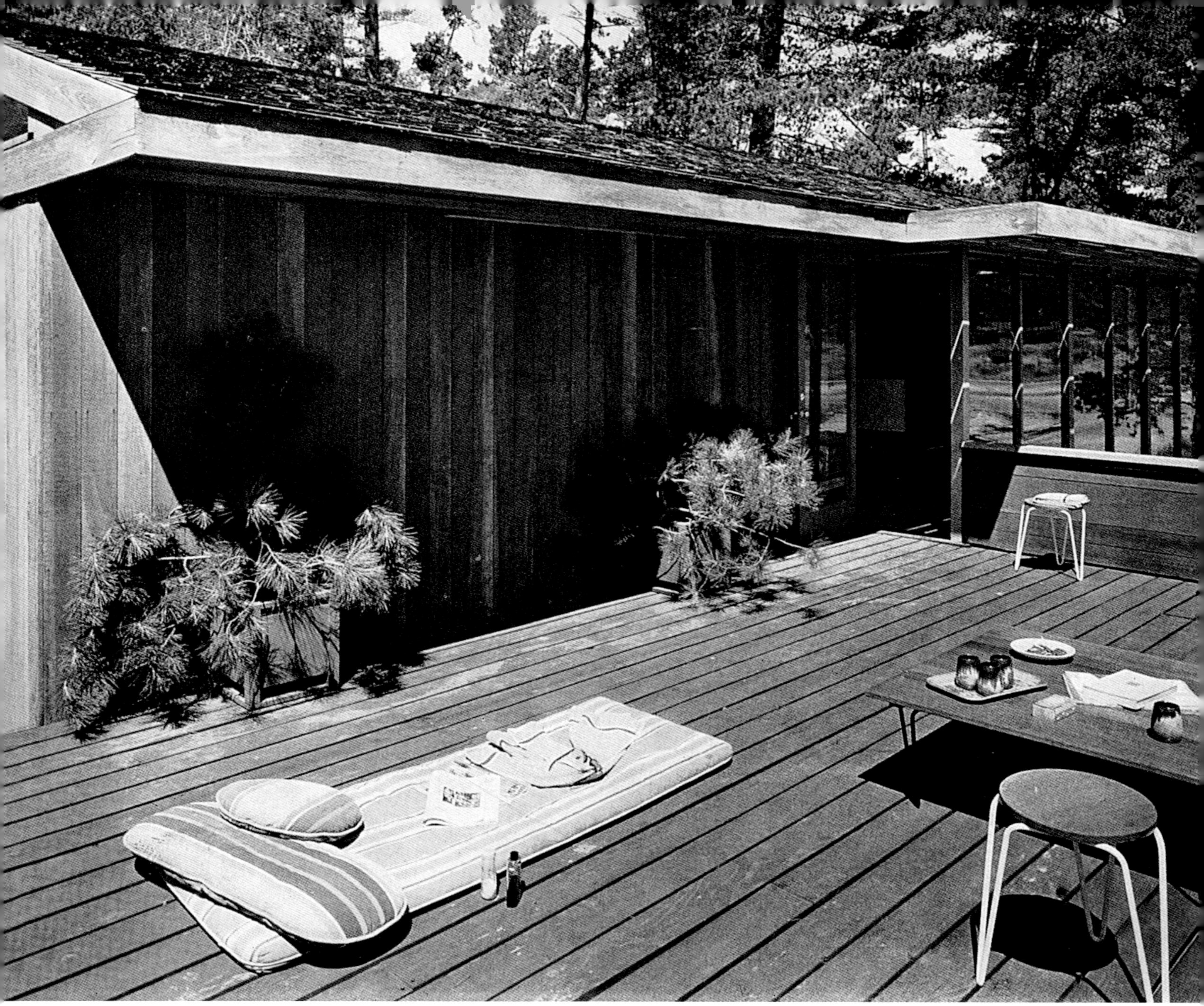

Drake's thoughts for a vacation house were "to provide a complete change of pace from everyday life . . . to be filled with surprises . . . and to offer as much individual choice of sun or shade, openness or intimacy, view or enclosure as possible." Decks (left) and terraces provide added luxury space for entertaining large groups of people.

View across living room (below) to sun deck and hills beyond. Panel in background can be moved to provide additional space for entertaining. Most of the interior finishes are stains or natural wood with a wax seal.

can be opened, slipped one way or another, or lifted out of their tracks and removed entirely . . . with additional curtains, one can turn the dining room into sleeping space for unexpected guests; a closet is provided for this possible use.

"The kitchen and bath are placed next to one another, and all fixtures are connected to the central plumbing core for economy. The bathroom is adjacent to the bedroom, living room, and auxiliary sleeping room and can be used without disturbing the privacy of any of the three. The kitchen is small but efficient, planned on the assumption that informality is one of the touchstones of a holiday.

"Both ends of the gable roof are opened with glass to give additional high light in the fireplace alcove and in the bedroom without sacrificing privacy. Provision is made for closing off the large bay window in the evening by drawing light draperies across them. Lighting between the glass and fabric is thrown down on the fabric in such a manner that a complete screen is made between inside and out; during the day, the light drapery would make a light filmy screen across the area.

"All lighting, direct and indirect, and all closets and cabinets are built in. In the living and sleeping rooms the floor is carpeted. Asphalt tile is used in the kitchen and bath. Walls are of redwood siding in the main area, plaster in the service unit. The beams and roof boards in the ceiling are exposed. Color is taken from nature: grey-green from the trees, light grey from the decomposed shale of the ground, deep black green from the pines, and soft yellow from the dried summer grass."

The studio office was the most intimate expression of Drake's work. He

Plan for Studio-Carmel. Building was designed as a basic unit that could be expanded as the need arose into a series of other related offices. During the time Drake lived in Carmel, it was used as his office; it later became a studio for a local artist; then it was partially remodeled for a living unit. Finally it was acquired by a young architect and his wife who faithfully restored the original conditions after they became interested in the story of Drake's Carmel Dream.

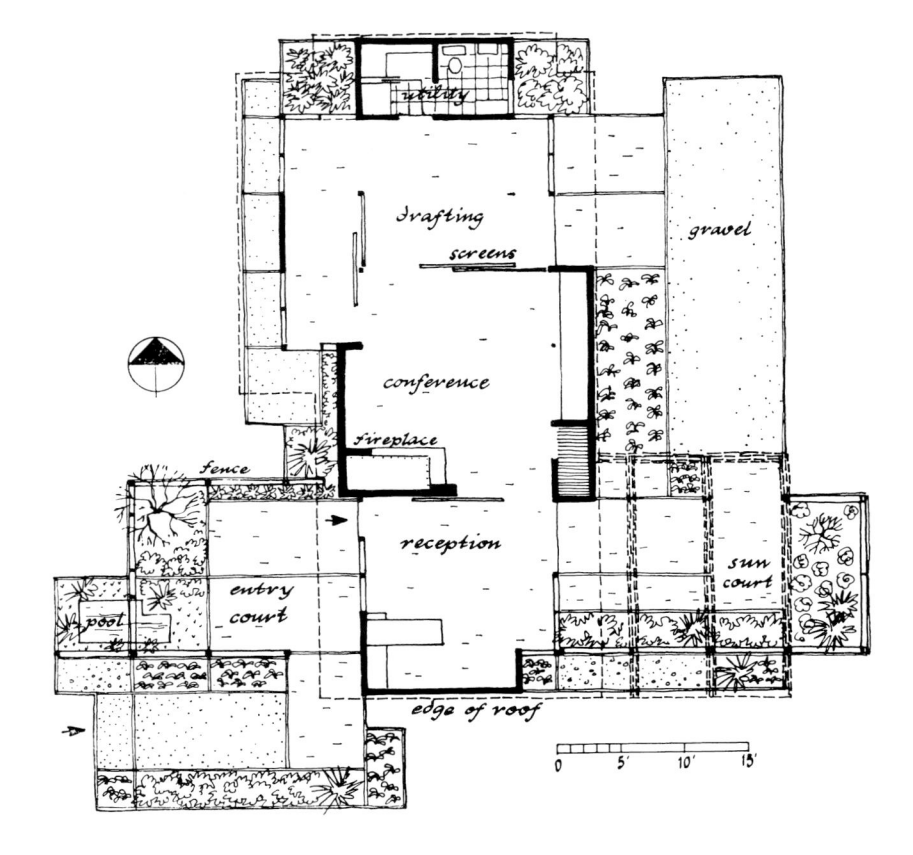

Approach (above) to studio entrance. Parking is on a lower level; a woodland path leads to the entry court where there is the first transition between nature and the building in the form of a redwood screen of changing pattern and form. The immediate view is directly through the structure to another terrace beyond.

Garden terrace (left) is a series of enclosures—some open, some closed—where privacy and protection are achieved without diminishing the scale of the outdoors. The overhead arbor is extended to hold adjustable screens for shade.

worked on it, day by day, from October to April. He knew how the winds shifted, how long the winter shadows were, where it was sheltered and warm, and he built it into the climatic cycle as he went.

The large main room could be divided into a reception area, a conference room, and an exhibition room. It was developed around the masonry mass of the fireplace. One wall contained storage cabinets and an exhibition panel on which displays of photographs, painting, sculpture were arranged.

A series of sliding screens separated the public room and the working parts; a workyard, bath, utility space and storage closets.

"The office works wonders on those who see it. It's perhaps the subtlest and wisest thing I could have done at the time, for it seems to create a mood on those who see it. After the landscaping has grown sufficiently to soften the newness, it will be a pleasant place to work."

Drake built three buildings in Carmel: the studio-office that was to be the

Entrance to studio (above) demonstrates the designer's ability to complete his design beyond the actual limits of the enclosed space of the building and still continue the pace of the structure.

Partial fence screen and garden pool terminating the entrance garden (left top). Plantings are of native material to keep the costs and the maintenance at a minimum.

Reverse view (left bottom) past the garden pool to the entry. The splash pool adds a sparkle to the shade of the giant oaks and madrones while providing a dipping pool for the watering pot.

Storage cabinet and display wall (right) for drawings, paintings, or sketch ideas; also a service counter for a hot plate and facilities for impromptu entertaining.

Fireplace alcove (below right) with large copper hood which actually supplied all the heat for the studio at first. Built-in couch provided a bed when the work continued through the night.

Receptionist desk and storage counter (below) by front entrance court. Flooring of brick on sand extends to garden terrace beyond; sand was to be later replaced with mortar joints.

beginning of the school, the Vacation House, and the Mesa house. The owners of the Mesa house wrote: "We are gloriously happy in this wonderful house. You will never know how vitally important it is. Thank you."

Drake thought for a time that by continuing private work in Carmel he might find a way to handle the school idea single-handed. But after an honest

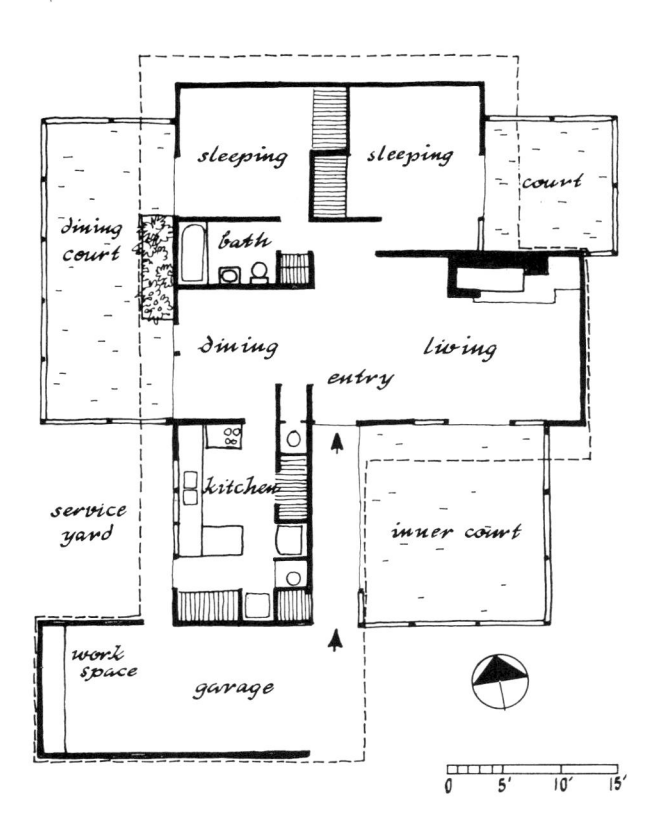

The Mesa house (left) in Carmel was designed for a builder who wanted to speculate on a non-typical two-bedroom home. Exterior redwood was treated with gray creosote stains with accents of black on the trim.

Drake felt this house failed in the scale of the garden courts (above right): "I think the important thing is to get away from the relationships of room sizes when you go into the garden."

(Below right) enclosed living room garden area is small and trim; it is possible to see and feel the distant hills by screening out the foreground distractions of houses and roads.

Dining room and outdoor terrace for mild weather entertaining (left). Although all the hall space was thrown into the living area, normal circulation leaves a quiet spot in the dining room.

Dining room terrace is shut away from the adjoining service yard (below left) and has full access to the bedroom to the north and total protection by the enclosing fence.

Northwest bedroom and terrace garden relationship (below). House has asphalt tile floors; the original slab floor lost its surface in an unexpected rainstorm.

Northeast bedroom and private terrace suitable for sunbathing or for children's outdoor "play pen" (right). Early morning light streams into this bedroom of the Mesa house.

Copper hood and raised hearth detail (below right) recurred in all three of the Carmel houses with slight variations to make them more efficient heating devices to offset the foggy weather.

Desk and bookcase unit placed in living room alcove with overhead spotlight built into the lighting trough (below). Redwood cabinet work was built and painted on the job.

appraisal of his assets, he realized that the Carmel chapter of his life was coming to a close.

On the plus side were the buildings. He felt he had built for the people, not for himself. "If I were to be called into the Marines tomorrow, I would feel all right leaving these last three buildings behind."

Also there was his relationship with Walter Doty of *Sunset Magazine*, published in San Francisco. In him he found an understanding ally. Doty not only gave him incentive ("A visit with Walter is like a shot in the arm," he said), but also gave him an opportunity to express himself in many ways—designing houses, cabins, and outdoor structures for *Sunset Magazine*.

At the final count, the projects outlined on his drawing board gave him the "small assurance that I have made progress in the last year."

But even so, it was difficult to keep the failure of his great Carmel dream from spreading its dark color over everything.

Certainly, Carmel without the school was not his place. To return to Los Angeles and forget his dream was unthinkable. Perhaps he could find a new road forward in San Francisco. He had good friends there—notably landscape architect Douglas Baylis. And San Francisco to him was a city that encouraged men with dreams.

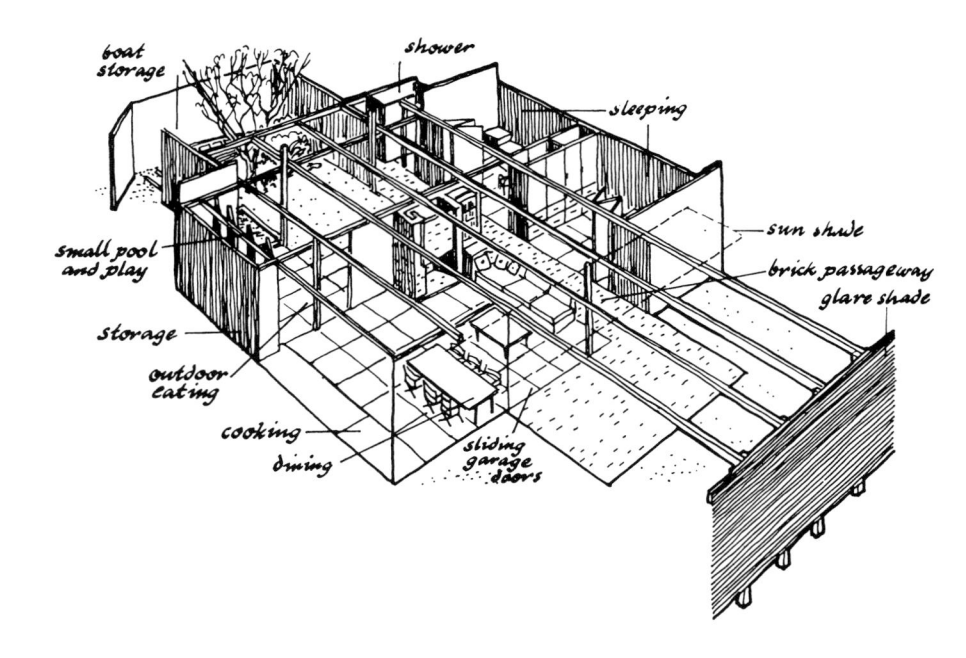

8 SAN FRANCISCO

Sketch of a western beach cabin designed for Sunset Magazine in 1950. A minimum cost structure that is in tune with its surroundings, it was planned for protection from the sun, wind, and glare, for easy maintenance. Brick passageway formed corridor for access without disturbing the main living areas of the house. Cabin had a fenced-in area for supervised play which could be locked during the off-season months. Sketch view is from the beach side.

In the fall of 1949 Drake moved to San Francisco and opened a small office on Washington Street. It was a slow time for architects.

Walter Doty at *Sunset* gave him as much editorial work as he could handle; he also commissioned him to do a *Sunset* house for the Pacific Central region. *Better Homes and Gardens* assigned some jobs in collaboration with Baylis. Such magazine work provided income for an architectural office, but it did not support it. Financially, it would soon be necessary for him to work for someone else.

It was a period of staring out of the window, waiting for work, marking time. The past seemed desirable ("Hell, I miss the good life of the sea and the pine tree . . . one day I'll get back there and make the idea stick"), the present unfocused, the future depressing. War was in the air; he expected to be called back for Korean service. He brooded over the conditions leading to wars, and his part in them.

"The only people who can be blamed for what we are now is ourselves. Each of us bears a measure of guilt for what has happened. Myself for wanting to come home and build houses, others for wanting to do something else

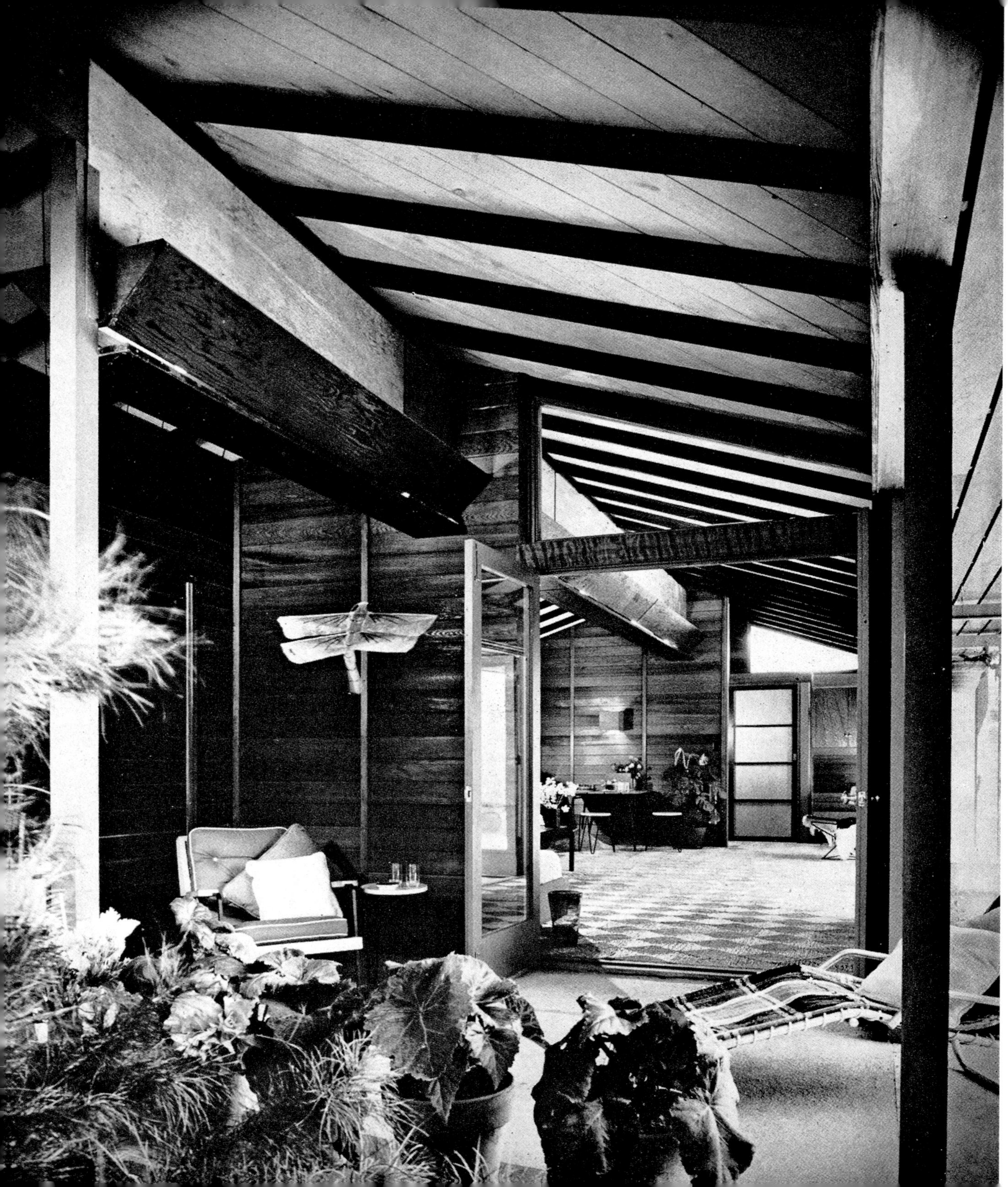

The Unit House was another experiment in modular construction of a 3' interval, which made for easy expansion and greater flexibility. This house was designed to grow from a one-room apartment to a final two-bedroom structure to take care of children. Drake designed the house to grow in its kitchen facilities as well as the living spaces. Additional roofed terraces for children's play under supervision from the kitchen was provided.

that was concerned with their own interests rather than with their place in this changing world. I guess it really goes further than that. . . . I hope we see this time that no man or nation is an island within himself. . . . I've had a hell of a wonderful life and I'm perfectly willing to go again to pay the toll on these last few years. . . . In one way, this period of change is one of the great adventures of civilization. Who knows, perhaps it's good that the idea of communism is making us re-examine what we believe in America. Perhaps materialism won't be so all-important when we're forced to look upon spiritual and moral values again. . . ."

In January 1951 he started to work for Architect Ernest J. Kump of San Francisco.

He wrote: "This sums up one era for me."

He kept his office at 619 Washington for evening and week-end work on his Carmel project—what he called the Drake "postwar" house. "If I ever get through this Korean thing, I'm going to build the most wonderful goddam house ever, and what's more I'm going to live in it! . . . I feel that I'm just coming to the time when I can make a real contribution to architecture. No matter where I go, or what I do, I shall be thinking and planning."

With the prospect of Marine recall still hovering over him, he worked for Kump daytimes, on his Carmel house evenings, and spent his week ends hiking and camping in the high Sierra.

The fall of 1951 marked the completion of two important projects: the Unit House designed jointly with Douglas Baylis, and the Malibu house planned in 1947; and the studies and sketches for Baylis' own remodel on Telegraph Hill in San Francisco.

The two houses are characterized by Drake's four basic approaches to modern domestic architecture: indoor-outdoor continuity, modular construction, architecturally-used light, and a sense of restraint.

The Unit House is based on a three-foot module, designed with the flexibility to expand from an original one-room apartment to a two-bedroom house. It contains five distinct zones for California outdoor living: a roofed terrace at the end of the living room, a sun terrace framed into a curved retaining wall, a shade terrace under a light trellis of wooden slats, a sheltered terrace protected from the wind by screens and planting, and a play terrace that can be supervised from the kitchen.

The Malibu house, on the boards when he was in Los Angeles, finally got under way while Drake was in San Francisco. Built on a cliff-edge some sixty feet above the beach, the house commands a tremendous sweeping view of the sea to the south, is backed by the low range of the Santa Lucia mountains

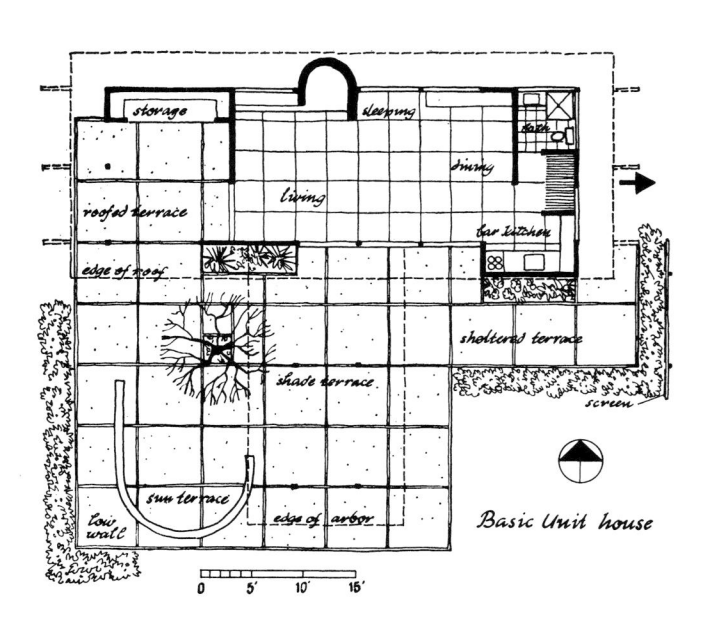

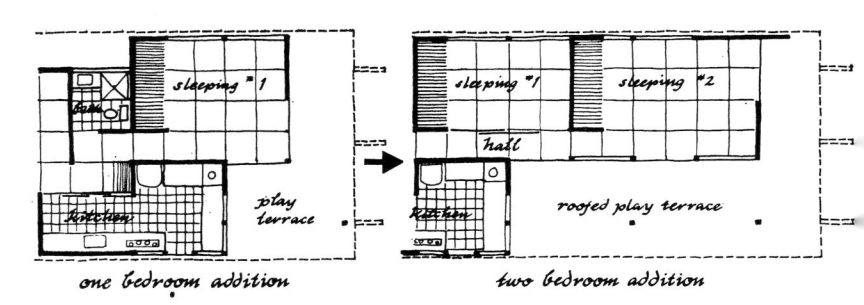

A small house that expands in stages, the Unit House (plans above) was built in the Bay Area in the fall of 1950 for $5,600, which included the terraces, arbor, and brick seat wall. To expand the house for an additional bedroom, Drake designed the nonstructural walls to be removed easily. The tiny kitchen expands with the addition of a bedroom and complete storage wall. The second bedroom can be added at any future time. This house, by virtue of its sheltering roof, has the ability to grow with the family and to use the garden as auxiliary living space through climate control and demonstrates that you can achieve luxury living for a minimum cost.

A view of the fireplace (left). The bed frames hold an ordinary box spring and mattress; the lighting box gives a direct light for reading. The fireplace hearth is concrete and with cushions makes pleasant extra sitting space.

View (right) toward the fireplace and onto the roofed porch that overlooks a small stream below. The bed couches are on rollers and swing out easily when they are to be made up. Lighting trough overhead, lined with copper foil, is constructed of light plywood panels and throws a warm coppery light up to the celotex ceiling above. Concrete slab is covered with sections of removable hemp matting which can be cleaned by hosing.

View (below) demonstrates the intimate relation between the house and the terrace. Exterior paving is concrete with water-washed concrete aggregate exposed to cut glare and prevent slipping. Redwood headers divide the area into 6 foot squares (double the house module). Banks of doors thrown wide to the garden area make it difficult to know where the house begins and the garden ends.

Malibu house with a screened garden room and brick-paved terrace makes a verdant retreat completely protected from the wind and glare of the sand and sea. The roof beams of the house carry from indoors to outdoors to organize the patio, fences, and trellises. Drake was concerned with never having a passage from shade to sun without a trellis or planting to soften the flow.

to the north. Every vista, from passage to glass door, from window to window to the great glass frontal southern wall, is seaward. There is a stillness within that is in direct contrast to the sight of the ever-restless moving sea. And yet there is rhythm in the construction; walls, cabinets, supporting posts and beams repeat the module design in the horizontal dimension. Sliding doors, panels, and garden screens bring seclusion and isolation within the sense of light, space, and openness. The sea and the mountains are brought inside through colors—again grey-greens, sand and brick tones. There's a unity of

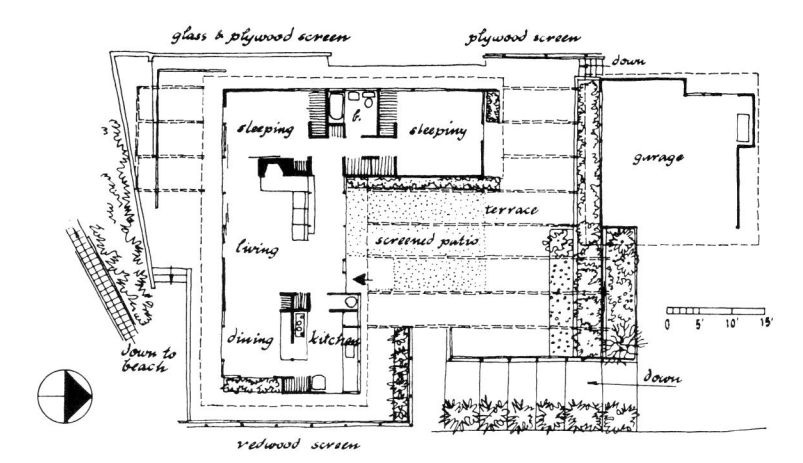

Colors follow the structural system of the house: beams and posts are painted black-green; sash and doors, grey-green; ceilings are sand color; interior and exterior walls are natural finish redwood; floor is cork. Shoji screens have stretched muslin and natural burlap with occasional inserts of rice paper for accent.

Sliding panels (above) can be moved with the sun to cut the glare anywhere in the living areas; windscreen beyond has fixed glass panels and occasional solid inserts, repeating the pattern of the forward shoji screens, painted bright colors in contrast with the sea.

View to living room from the dining area (left). Built-in buffet and cabinets in dining room open into the kitchen area. Record player and storage units are at end of the casework.

Living room (above) opens directly to the screened garden room. Lighting throughout the Malibu house is by continuous soffits of various widths mounted at door heights.

View from the kitchen to the sea (right top) shows the food preparation center, the telephone, and the herb shelf. Service door has immediate access to the paved areas surrounding the house.

The lowered-ceiling corridor (right bottom) appears in several Drake houses to handle traffic without disturbing the main core. Bookcase baffle pierced by dark-stained posts gives drama to the entrance opposite.

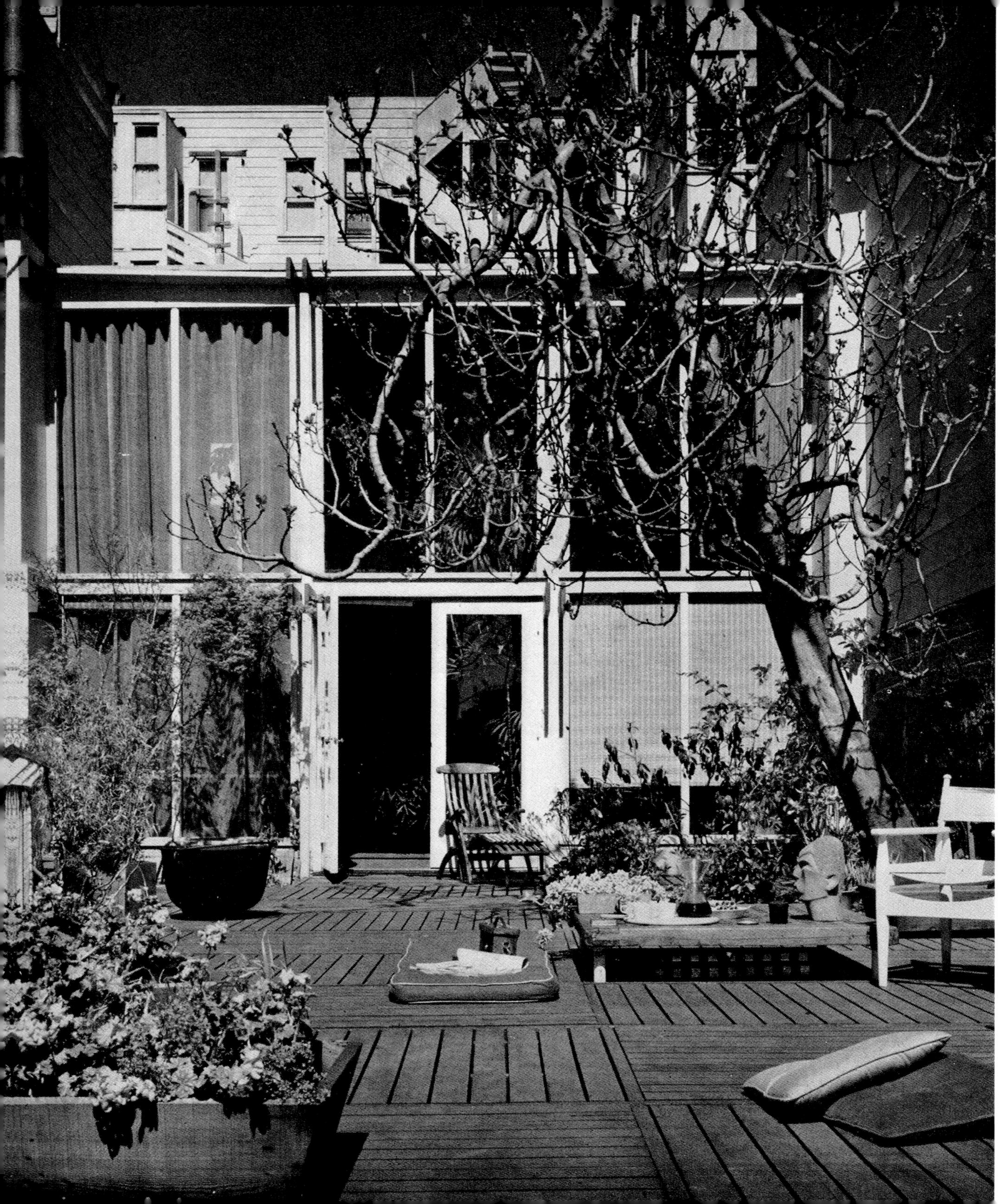

Detail shot (above) showing portion of the structural system on the upper floor of the Baylis house. This was Drake's last project and his only remodeling job.

South elevation of remodeled Baylis house in San Francisco, California (left). Essentially a two-story glass cage sandwiched between old wood structures on the west side of Telegraph Hill and built to enclose an office-studio and living quarters, the owners can enjoy the garden while at their desks.

The remodeling was started in May of 1951 and continued on a do-it-yourself-basis until the Fall of 1956 with the owner's father-in-law, Fred Hilbiber, the only real workman on the job. The house project and this memorial publication to Gordon Drake serve as a constant reminder to them of his contribution to their way of life.

View of the first floor office-studio (right) Redwood block flooring, spiral stair, interior planting, and work table. Colors are dark blue frame contrasted with off-white walls.

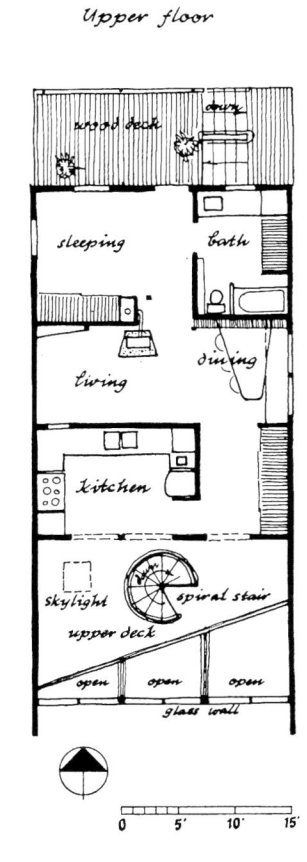

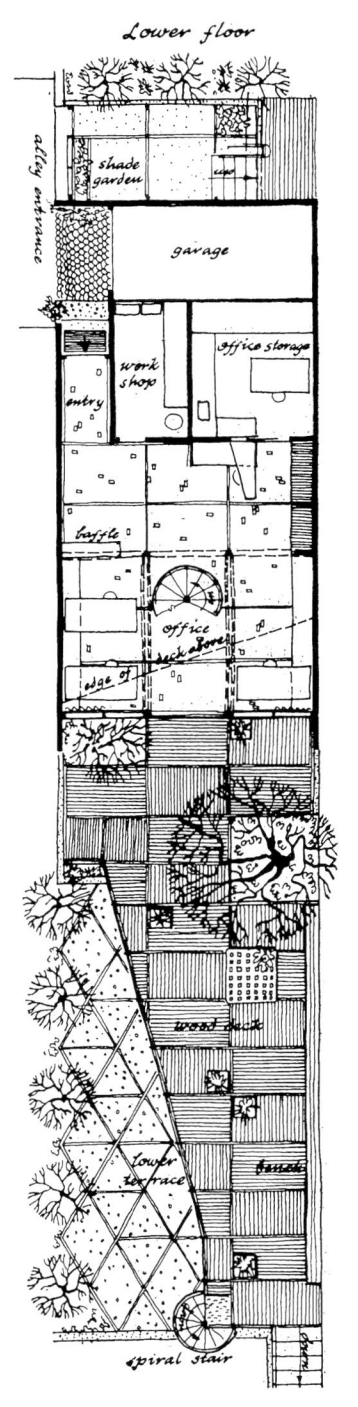

house, site, land, and sea that makes this house perhaps his most comprehensive and characteristic piece of work.

"It's good," he wrote to Sanderson in New York, after one of his week ends in the Sierra, "to see things that are changeless. There's a wonderful spirit about the mountains and the sea. If I seem overly philosophic it's only because when one thinks that a great change is about to take place, there's a very keen appreciation of the here and now."

In another letter: "I wish I knew of a better way to express a belief in freedom than by reaching for the nearest gun, but until I do find a better way, it must suffice. Perhaps this only proves that you really care for something when you are about to lose it."

And, later, "I've had a pretty wonderful life. For the most part I've always worked for things I believed in. . . . In architecture I've never knowingly drawn a dishonest line. . . . It's been a good life. Perhaps you have to pay for that kind of living, if you want it to continue. . . ."

In late summer he wrote to a friend that for the moment he was feeling peaceful. "Perhaps it's because the human being isn't capable of being forever kept on the knife-edge of indecision. Suddenly I'm no longer so terribly excited about the Korean war and the state of the world."

In September he had word from the Marines: they wanted him for a month, and only a month. On his return, he became absorbed and excited by a new commission. He decided to take the State architectural examinations.

He wrote, "As soon as the examinations are over, I plan to take off for a few days' skiing. So the next letter you get will probably be written from a nice comfortable hospital bed. . . ."

January of 1952 was a time of severe snowstorms, a time when few ventured to reach the snowbound lodges in the Sierra. January 15 dawned bright and clear after a week end of crippling storms and a record snowfall. Drake and his two companions, restless during the blizzard which had confined them two extra days at the ski resort, were eager to get out into the soft powdered snow.

"Like an ardent life," John Muir had written years before, "this day was full of very bright and very dark places." It was the day that Gordon Drake died halfway down the mountain slope.

Gordon Drake now lies in the Military Cemetery on the high land of Point Loma near San Diego in company with thousands of his fellow Marines. It is a place which commands one of the great seascapes of the world, a vast panorama of ocean, bays, islands, mountains, and plains. From there you may look across the border into Mexico.

Many who knew Drake only by his work, who had never met him personally, were deeply affected by his death. Those who knew and respected him must have felt as he did at the death of his brother Max during World War II: "It was an immense privilege to have known him as long as we did, and like everyone and everything else mere death does not destroy . . . there is no connection between a headstone in a military cemetery and the man that we knew."

Over and over again, Gordon Drake declared that it was his avowed intention to design decent houses for people on minimum budgets. It is natural enough, therefore, that he will be best remembered for his small houses designed for California living.

One kind of assessment of his work can be approached through looking at the things he used.

He used light as an integral element of the structure, a device to stress a particular point in composition or in space. He brought in natural light from outside through clerestories, glass gable ends, translucent screens, glass walls. He captured and controlled artificial light in recessed frames, behind opaque panels, in directioned troughs.

Manipulating light, he furnished his houses with moods. He used screens to block off moments of solitude, enclosing an area within a room or in the garden with portable seclusion. He used panels as backdrops to frame plant structure, to suspend in shadow movement a momentary breeze. He used the gentleness of diffused light for inwardness, the probing of morning's bright light for expansiveness.

But perhaps the material he used best—because only he could use it—was his struggle in the seven years he practiced professionally—1945 to 1952—to define and communicate his own values. He was working with human values—handled, through his work, in terms of the particular client's desires. His questionnaire, headed "What are your requirements?" said in part:

"It should be understood that any attempt to design a house which would be perfectly suited to your requirements and be esthetically pleasing must necessarily be in the nature of a compromise, since economic considerations and space limitations are usually governing factors. For example, a large and completely equipped kitchen might seem desirable, but might result in reducing areas in other parts of the house. This questionnaire is, therefore, an attempt to determine the relative importance of the various spaces of the house as they relate to your needs and desires."

To try to measure his contribution to architecture is to try to measure the intangibles with which he worked. Every man who has ever dreamed of building a house deals with his own intangibles; he must question, at one level or another, the things that are important to enclose within it. Every builder or architect who has ever built a house must try to open up the lines of communication to arrive at his client's intangibles, and every builder or architect will impose upon his structures, knowingly or unknowingly, some of his own.

Perhaps the best estimate of Drake's work can be arrived at through the recognition that in the very smallness of the things he appreciated most—the green grass, a breeze across a body, an untainted blue sky—is their largeness. Each bit of human experience, recognized and found valuable and passed on, is one more piece among the many millions of pieces in the total pattern of the relationship between man, his shelter, and his environment.

Carl Birger Troedsson
Arkitekt, Docent
Hovås, Sweden

The class of architectural students to which Gordon belonged at the University of Southern California was an interesting, stimulating one. The years were depression years, the depression-ridden years that so many try to gloss over and forget.

To the already restless and searching youth was added the worry of the uncertainty as to their future—work for graduates of architectural schools was non-existent. To the architectural students, at least at U. S. C., they were hard years—the struggle to find money for tuition and for the daily meal was a very serious one; all of that, however, seemed to be compensated for with the interest that they showed in their study of architecture. One cannot hope to find often such a group of interested and fine young men.

As in all schools of all times, I suppose, that class showed the individuals who were merely trying to get through, more or less impatient to get out into the world and wrestle a living out of architecture; and a more searching minority—and that minority in Gordon's class was particularly searching and particularly serious about its search and pursued it with great intent.

It searched its elders . . . their behavior and the world that they had left for the youth of the day; it searched the people who were preaching at the old stand. And when they found what they were searching for, then a chord responded in their own makeup, a tune had been struck which drew them and it was the strength of the appeal of the tune that was to decide their whole future.

In that class there were many who were holding their hands cupped to their ears—intent, purposeful, their eyes opening with a new understanding —and one of the most intent, serious and searching was Gordon. He became more absorbed as time went on, and his eyes opened even more until he was beginning to behold his innermost self struggling to greater heights. The instrument being played was mighty—"you just touch one string and the whole heavens ring"—still, out of the torments of the soul would surely come a purified spirit.

Then came the war and the youth struggling to find himself in the creativeness of building in a peaceful world rose to that also. Gordon came to see me before he left for the Pacific with the Marines. He was still intent and serious, and the prospect of death was in his mind. Should he not return, then he would like to have the money from his insurance used for some purpose which would further the cause of architecture. We spoke about that, but I could only assure him that he would come back from the Pacific where he was to spend years, like many others, far removed from the creative struggle he had contemplated. Fortunately it was possible during those years to dream about architecture, and the letters to friends told much of how a young man comes through the process of dreaming about creating and constructing a better world—and killing the enemy at the same time.

But, instead of in the Pacific, it was in the high Sierra that his life ended much too soon.

I salute the idealistic, intent, serious young people in Gordon Drake.

Harwell Hamilton Harris
Architect
Fort Worth, Texas

I knew Gordon first as a student. He was one of twelve in a class at the University of Southern California in 1940 when I was a summer critic there. We criticized the other work he had done as much as what he did for my class. I don't recall his finishing any of the drawings. When satisfied there was nothing further to be discovered by continuing a design, he dropped it. Knowing this about him, it is surprising that I let him come to work for me in the fall.

Among the jobs in the office at this time were the Havens house in Berkeley, the Birtcher house in Los Angeles and the Lek house in La Jolla. But the Fellowship Park house, built six years earlier, held more meaning for him than any still on the boards. Perhaps it was because this was one of my first buildings that it spoke so directly to Gordon. He was already absorbed in modular design and panel construction. What the Fellowship Park house had in addition was rhythmic organization of panels and a continuous frame structure. The panels were in groups of two, which immediately changed the rhythm from a monotonous march to something approaching a dance; by sliding the right member of each pair of panels in front of the left member, a series of one-two steps was produced; by sliding first the right and then the left in the series of pairs, a still more complex rhythm appeared; by alternating glass panels with cloth panels, with Celotex panels, with no panels, still more complicated rhythms were achieved. By dividing the unit into one-third units with which to parallel, oppose and pace the full units and double units, an effect of depth was produced. The continuous structural frames were the consequence of using not one but several members to make up a column, a girder, a floor beam and, by dropping some members of each at an intersection, allowing the others to continue through. Each of the members was kept distinct by offsetting or spacing so that visual continuity was retained.

Here was the principle guiding design and Gordon was quick to see it. It absorbed him because of its implications. Here mind and spirit and the kind of order existing in nature might find architectural expression. Architectural expressiveness was apparently what he was looking for. Visiting the Havens job in Berkeley during its construction, he saw Bernard Maybeck's Christian Science Church for the first time. Here was a building more expressive than any he had seen before and one he could not forget.

After the war he was again in the office, which was now next to the Fellowship Park house. The office had the same continuous frame as the house, and Gordon arrived in time to supervise some of the construction. He also worked on drawings for a portable house and something else we called the Tool & Tea House—a ten-foot square segmental building with a petal roof.

He bought a lot and during outside office hours revised the plans of a house for himself whose design he had worked on throughout the whole of the period he was in the Pacific or at Camp Pendleton. Every few months I had received a print of the latest edition. Now, with the help of a young engineer he had met in the war and some of the other young draftsmen in the office, he built the house, working nights and week ends. The house was co-winner of the *Progressive Architecture* Award for private residences completed during 1946 that best exemplified sound design progress; despite low cost, it achieved the living amenity of a house many times its size.

Gordon was too full of ideas demanding immediate expression to wait for opportunities to appear in order to build them. And he felt sure that he could find a way to bring the small house within the reach of the young war veteran whose need he apparently felt bound to heed. So he left the office to design and build.

Except for the four or five years of the war which he spent in the Marines, architecture absorbed him fully. In a way, the experience forced upon him as an officer in charge of landing operations in his group only deepened this absorption. The recurring sight of boys' lives being sacrificed drove him to find relief by transferring his thoughts elsewhere. For the insanity of the world about him he substituted the perfection of the world of architecture. Architecture grew to encompass all that is great and noble and shining. It became the star that brought him back from the war.

He was impatient with the interruption of the war, he was impatient with his own slowness, he was impatient with the unwillingness of others to understand. He was confident that architecture was the way: that as he reached simplicity and unity and meaning in architecture he would reach them in his own life. Design became discovery and working out the consequences of discovery. Continuity became the reality. He was only started when he died.

Walter L. Doty
Director of Editorial Research
Sunset Magazine
Menlo Park, California

One single idea tore at Gordon Drake when I knew him.

He felt that architecture was without meaning until it was used. The publication of a prize-winning house meant very little unless it brought about the designing of thousands of houses. Architecture, to fulfill its destiny, must be used by all the people who build.

The dream of an architectural center in Carmel grew out of this deep inner drive. He had to try to find a way to make the purchase of architectural service as normal as the purchase of any other service. He was angered by the fact that the talented graduate of an architectural school could not make a living practising in the small town. The need for talent in design was everywhere, while the talented went hungry.

The idea that architecture should be used by everyone disciplined his own work. The ideas he exposes do not require high costs per square foot, nor do the principles need detailed blue-printing to be applied. Gordon was a carpenter as well as a designer. His first designs were created to be carried out by amateur builders. In none of his subsequent work is this first simplicity forgotten.

This book had to be published to carry out Gordon's desire to bring design to everyone.

ACKNOWLEDGMENTS:

Julius Shulman: for photos of Drake's own house, Spillman, Presley, Dammann, the model of the Carmel studio, the Malibu, and the Basic Unit houses;

Morley Baer: for photos of Vacation House, Carmel studio, Mesa house, and Baylis remodel;

Sunset Magazine: Lane Publishing Company, for loaning the color plates in this book;

Maggie Baylis: the wife of Douglas Baylis, for sketches, layout, and technical production of the book;

George A. Sanderson: Feature Editor, *Progressive Architecture*, for his help and encouragement; and for the loan of his correspondence from Drake which contained the written record of architectural hopes and dreams;

Walter L. Doty: *Sunset Magazine*, for editorial consultation and criticism; and for his statement of faith in Drake's architectural talents;

Carl Troedsson: architect and lecturer, for his inspiration to Drake's early progress;

Harwell Hamilton Harris: architect, for his sensitive analysis of Drake's architectural philosophy;

Betsy Roeth Kaplan: for typing and editing the biography;

William Stimmell: designer and former student under Drake, for technical assistance;

Jane Fylling: for biographical data concerning the Carmel phase;

Peggy Walls: for reviewing and editing;

Warren Radford: architect, for his interest and aid;

and finally, to

Pearl Drake Hunter: Gordon Drake's mother, for her whole-hearted devotion to this memorial and to the scholarship fund to be set up in the name of her son at the University of Southern California, Los Angeles.

The three vertical sections on these pages were selected from a vast file of Gordon Drake's working drawings. Details were set up on "standard" sheets, including the post sections appearing at the bottom of pages 89 and 90, to be used over and over again. About a hundred of these standards were completed.

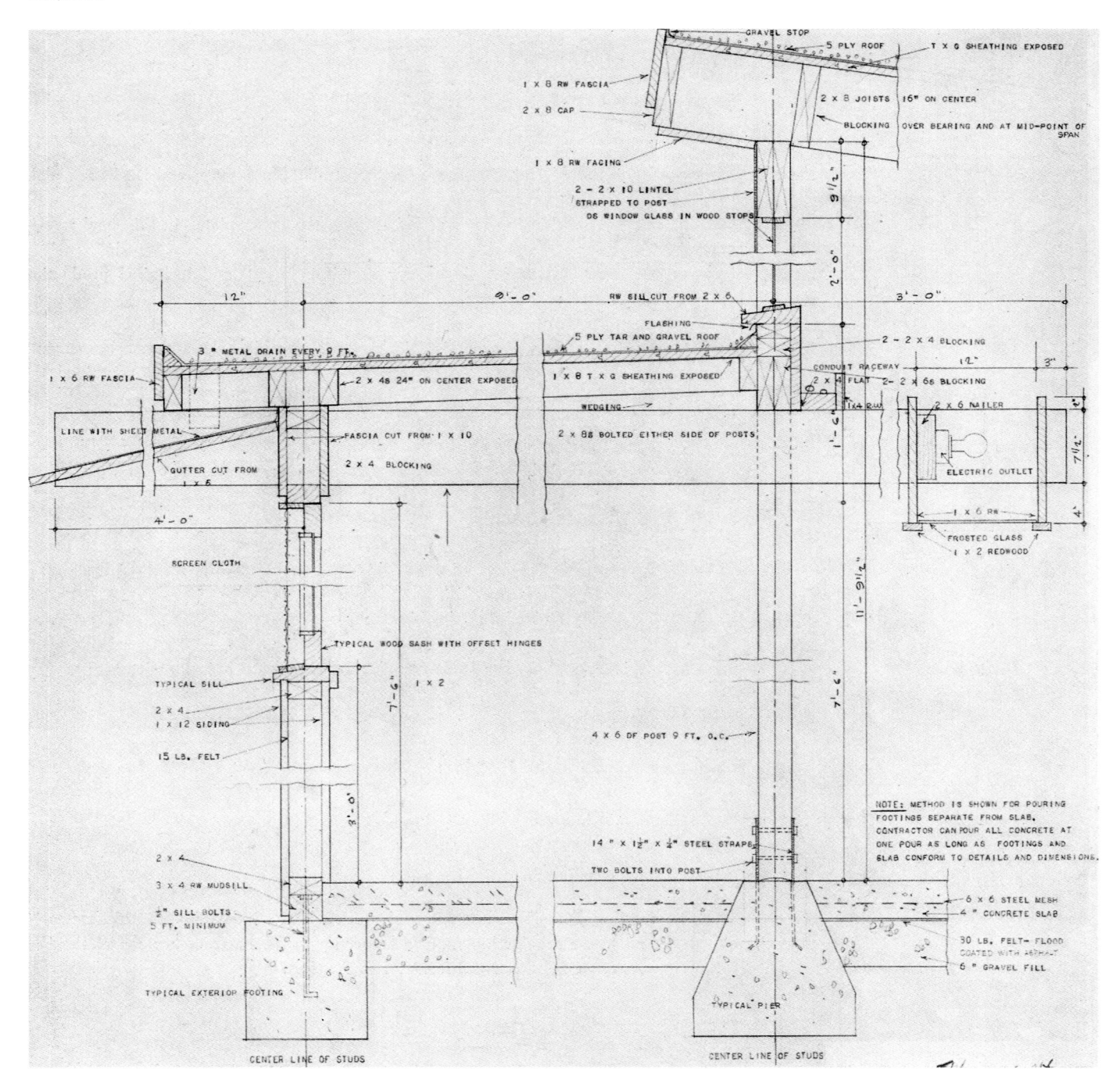

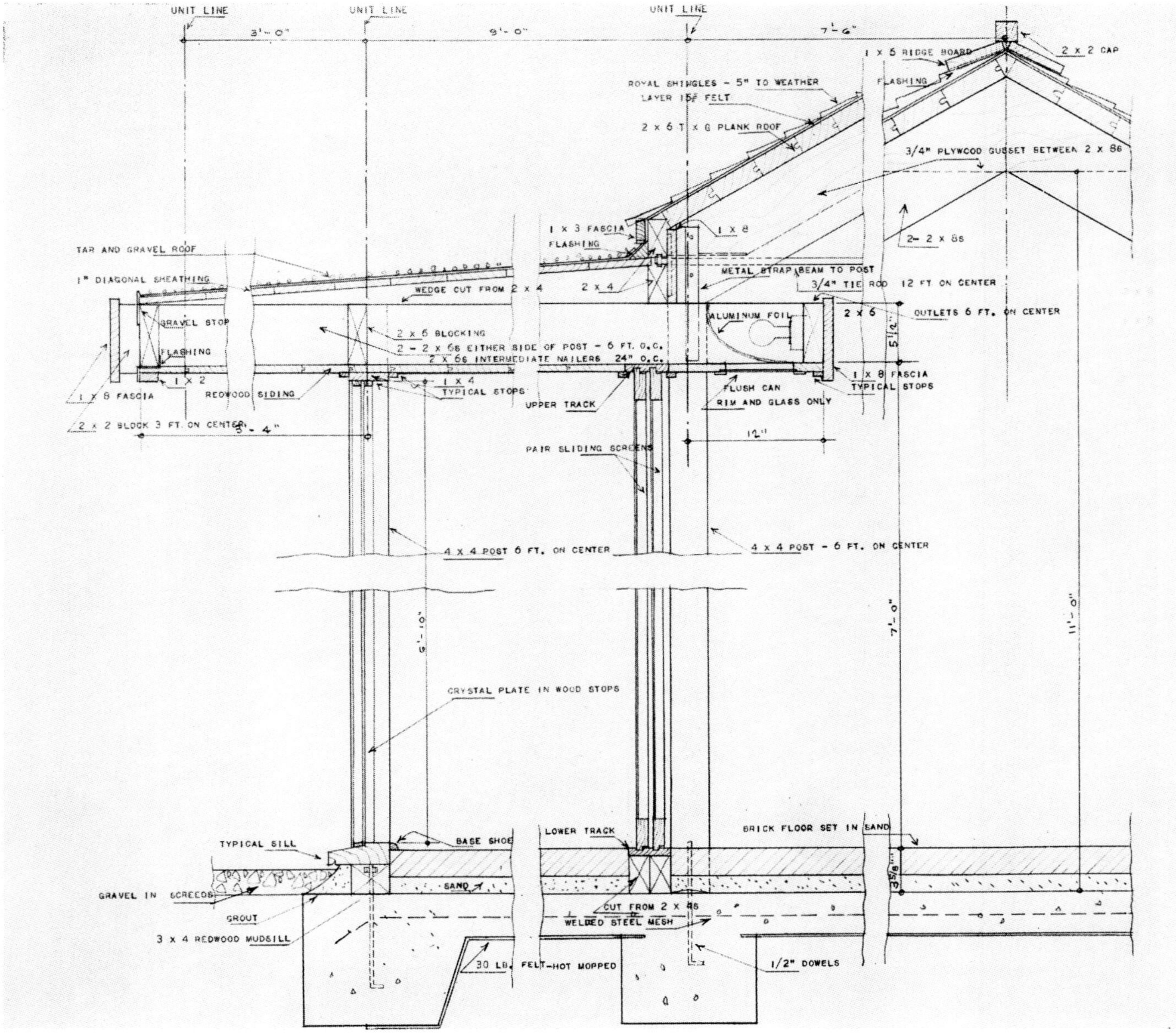
UNIT LINE
UNIT LINE
UNIT LINE
3'-0"
9'-0"
7'-6"
1 x 5 RIDGE BOARD
2 x 2 CAP
FLASHING
ROYAL SHINGLES - 5" TO WEATHER
LAYER 15# FELT
2 x 6 T x G PLANK ROOF
3/4" PLYWOOD GUSSET BETWEEN 2 x 8S
1 x 3 FASCIA
FLASHING
1 x 8
2- 2 x 8s
TAR AND GRAVEL ROOF
1" DIAGONAL SHEATHING
METAL STRAP BEAM TO POST
2 x 4
3/4" TIE ROD 12 FT ON CENTER
WEDGE CUT FROM 2 x 4
GRAVEL STOP
ALUMINUM FOIL
2 x 6
OUTLETS 6 FT. ON CENTER
2 x 6 BLOCKING
FLASHING
2 - 2 x 6s EITHER SIDE OF POST - 6 FT. O.C.
2 x 6s INTERMEDIATE NAILERS 24" O.C.
5 1/2"
1 x 2
1 x 4
1 x 8 FASCIA
TYPICAL STOPS
1 x 8 FASCIA
REDWOOD SIDING
TYPICAL STOPS
FLUSH CAN
UPPER TRACK
RIM AND GLASS ONLY
2 x 2 BLOCK 3 FT. ON CENTER
5'-4"
12"
PAIR SLIDING SCREENS
4 x 4 POST 6 FT. ON CENTER
4 x 4 POST - 6 FT. ON CENTER
5'-10"
7'-0"
11'-0"
CRYSTAL PLATE IN WOOD STOPS
TYPICAL SILL
BASE SHOE
LOWER TRACK
BRICK FLOOR SET IN SAND
GRAVEL IN SCREEDS
SAND
3 5/8"
GROUT
CUT FROM 2 x 4s
WELDED STEEL MESH
3 x 4 REDWOOD MUDSILL
30 LB. FELT-HOT MOPPED
1/2" DOWELS

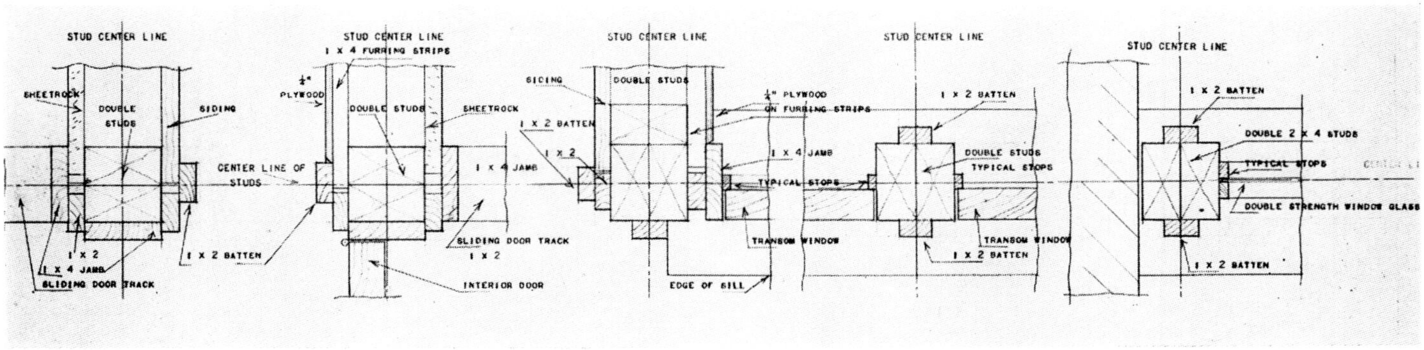
STUD CENTER LINE
STUD CENTER LINE
STUD CENTER LINE
STUD CENTER LINE
STUD CENTER LINE
SHEETROCK
DOUBLE STUDS
SIDING
1 x 4 FURRING STRIPS
1/4" PLYWOOD
DOUBLE STUDS
SHEETROCK
SIDING
DOUBLE STUDS
1/4" PLYWOOD ON FURRING STRIPS
1 x 2 BATTEN
1 x 2 BATTEN
DOUBLE 2 x 4 STUDS
1 x 2 BATTEN
1 x 2
1 x 4 JAMB
DOUBLE STUDS
TYPICAL STOPS
TYPICAL STOPS
CENTER LINE OF STUDS
1 x 4 JAMB
TYPICAL STOPS
DOUBLE STRENGTH WINDOW GLASS
1 x 2
1 x 4 JAMB
SLIDING DOOR TRACK
1 x 2 BATTEN
SLIDING DOOR TRACK
1 x 2
INTERIOR DOOR
TRANSOM WINDOW
EDGE OF SILL
TRANSOM WINDOW
1 x 2 BATTEN
1 x 2 BATTEN

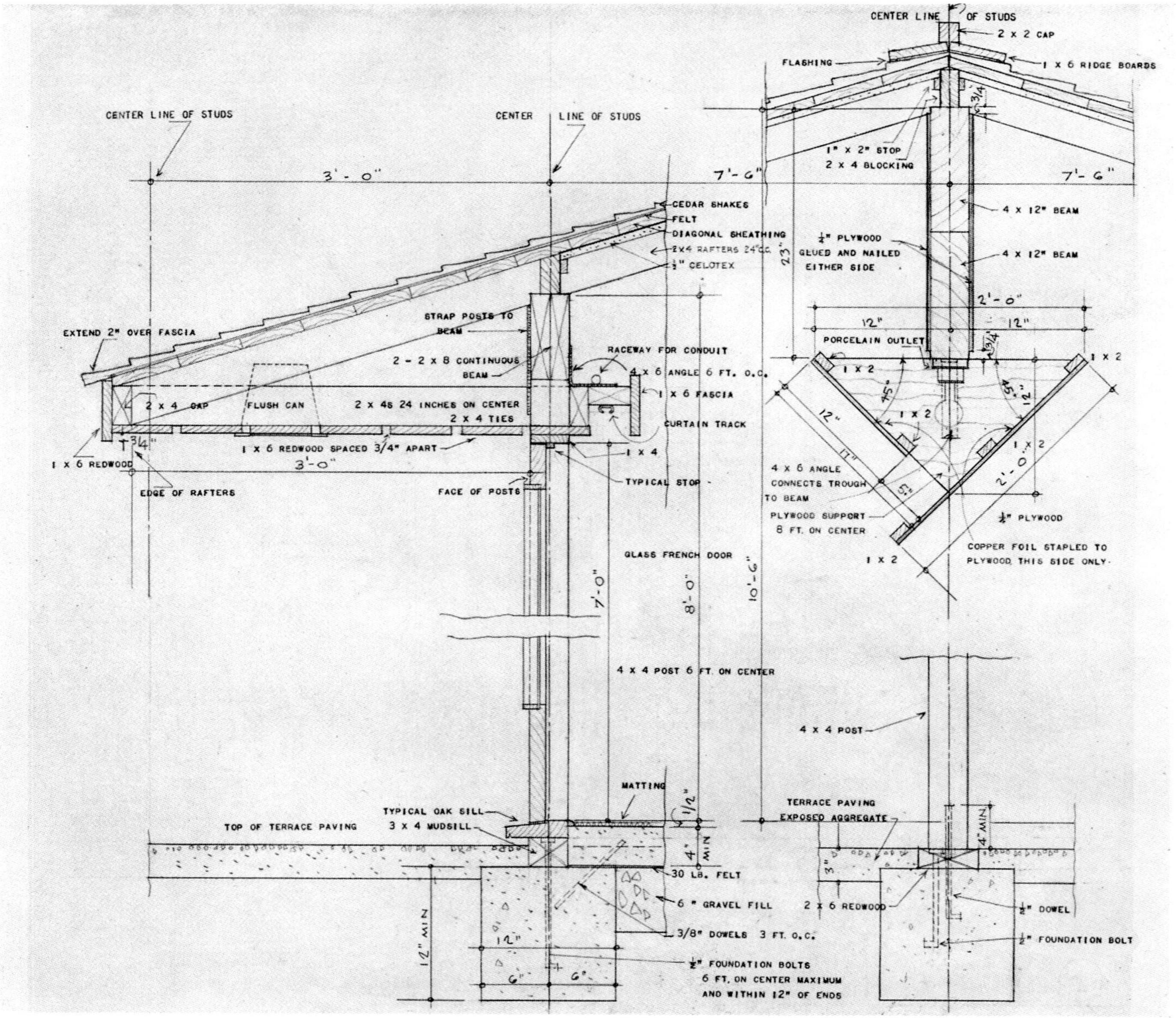
CENTER LINE OF STUDS
CENTER LINE OF STUDS
3'-0"
7'-6"
7'-6"
CEDAR SHAKES
FELT
DIAGONAL SHEATHING
2x4 RAFTERS 24" O.C.
½" CELOTEX
2 x 2 CAP
FLASHING
1 x 6 RIDGE BOARDS
1" x 2" STOP
2 x 4 BLOCKING
4 x 12" BEAM
½" PLYWOOD GLUED AND NAILED EITHER SIDE
4 x 12" BEAM
EXTEND 2" OVER FASCIA
STRAP POSTS TO BEAM
2 - 2 x 8 CONTINUOUS BEAM
RACEWAY FOR CONDUIT
4 x 6 ANGLE 6 FT. O.C.
1 x 6 FASCIA
CURTAIN TRACK
2 x 4 CAP
FLUSH CAN
2 x 4s 24 INCHES ON CENTER
2 x 4 TIES
1 x 6 REDWOOD SPACED 3/4" APART
1 x 6 REDWOOD
EDGE OF RAFTERS
1 x 4
TYPICAL STOP
FACE OF POSTS
PORCELAIN OUTLET
1 x 2
4 x 6 ANGLE CONNECTS TROUGH TO BEAM
PLYWOOD SUPPORT 8 FT. ON CENTER
½" PLYWOOD
COPPER FOIL STAPLED TO PLYWOOD THIS SIDE ONLY.
GLASS FRENCH DOOR
7'-0"
8'-0"
10'-6"
4 x 4 POST 6 FT. ON CENTER
4 x 4 POST
MATTING
TYPICAL OAK SILL
3 x 4 MUDSILL
TOP OF TERRACE PAVING
30 LB. FELT
6" GRAVEL FILL
3/8" DOWELS 3 FT. O.C.
½" FOUNDATION BOLTS 6 FT. ON CENTER MAXIMUM AND WITHIN 12" OF ENDS
TERRACE PAVING EXPOSED AGGREGATE
2 x 6 REDWOOD
½" DOWEL
½" FOUNDATION BOLT
12" MIN
4" MIN

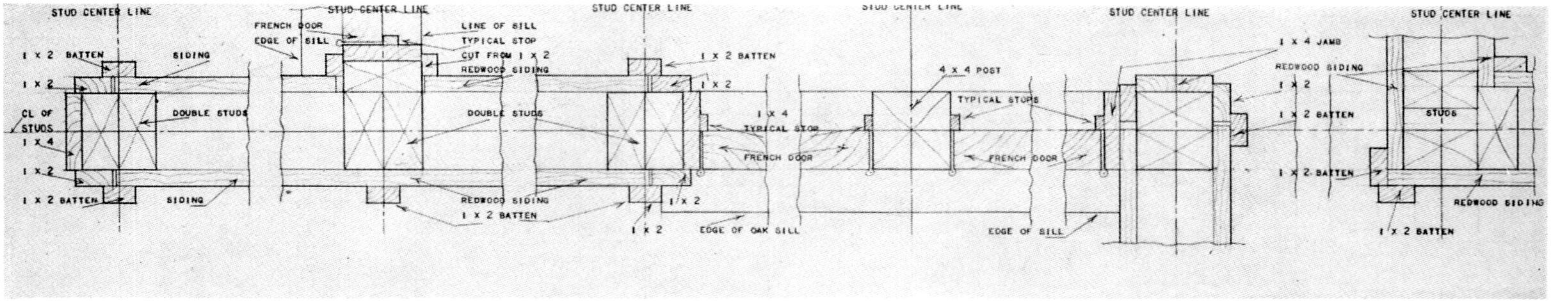
STUD CENTER LINE
1 x 2 BATTEN
SIDING
1 x 2
CL OF STUDS
1 x 4
DOUBLE STUDS
1 x 2 BATTEN
FRENCH DOOR
EDGE OF SILL
LINE OF SILL
TYPICAL STOP
CUT FROM 1 x 2
REDWOOD SIDING
DOUBLE STUDS
REDWOOD SIDING
1 x 2 BATTEN
1 x 4
TYPICAL STOP
FRENCH DOOR
EDGE OF OAK SILL
4 x 4 POST
TYPICAL STOPS
EDGE OF SILL
1 x 4 JAMB
STUDS

INDEX

Architectural Forum, 28,31
Awards, architectural, 16,22,23,25,31,84

Bachelor's house, studies for, 24-25
Baer, Frances, 55
Baylis, Douglas, 51,66,67,69
Beach cabin, sketch for, 66,67
Better Homes and Gardens, 67
Boylin, John, 47,51
Built-in furniture, 18,21,22,31,35,38,39,
  57,59,61,65,72

Cabin, beach, sketch for, 67
Cabin, mountain, sketch for, 28,29
California climate, architecture for,
  11,13,15-16,28,29,59,79
Carmel studio office, 48-50,57-61
Christian Science Church, 84
Clerestory windows, 18,28,38,42,80

Dammann house, 42-45
Doty, Walter, 66,67,85
Drake, Max, 9,10,79
Drake "postwar" house, 69

Fellowship Park house, 83,84
Form (Sweden), 22

Haleakala Theatre, 12-13
Harris, Harwell Hamilton, 10,83
Hilbiber, Fred, 77
HomeOla Corporation, 39
House and Garden, 25,31

Kump, Ernest J., 69

Labor, unskilled, 22,36,37,48,85
Lamb, Walter, 51
L'Architecture d'Aujord'hui, 22
Light, planning for, 28,31,33,34,38,41,42,45,
  52,57,59,65,72,74,80
Los Angeles, Calif. (postwar), 24-25
Los Angeles house, first, 14-22,84

Los Angeles house, second, 30
Low-cost housing, 6,16,22,31,36,39,67,79,84

Malibu house, 2(Col.Pl.),25,69,72-75
Marine veterans, employment of, 13,16
Mass produced units, 37,39,42
Maui, theatre at, 13
Maybeck, Bernard, 84
Mesa house, 19 (Col. Pl.),62-65
Midwest house, sketch for, 26
Modular construction, 37,69,70,83
Mountain cabin, sketch for, 28,29
Muir, John, 78

Neutra, Richard, 31

Outdoors, relation of houses to, 6,10,16,17,18,
  21,22,29,30,33,34,35,43,44,45,59,60,63,69,71,72

Panel construction, 36,37,39,41,55,57,59,74,83-84
Prefabricated units, 36,39
Postwar house, first, 14-22
Presley house, 25,31,36-42
Progressive Architecture, 16,22,23,25,84

Sanderson, George A., 7-8,23,24,51,78
Shoji panels, 20,55,73,74
Shulman, Julius, 18
Sites, influence of, 18,22,28,30,35,36,37,42,78
Soffits, lighting, 34,75
Soltanoff, Louis, 13,16,22
Spillman house, 25,31-35
Studio office, Carmel, 48-50,57-61
Stutz, William, 47,51
Sunset Magazine, 28,66,67

Theatre at Maui, 13
Tool & Tea House, 84
Troedsson, Carl Birger, 10,81

Unit House, 6,68-71
University of Southern California, 10,47,81-82

Vacation House, 52-57

Second Edition © 2011 by William Stout Publishers

All reproduction rights reserved.

Printed in China

Library of Congress Control Number 2010935369
ISBN 978-0-9795508-8-1

William Stout Publishers
1326-1328 S. 51st Street
Richmond, CA 94804
www.stoutpublishers.com

The publication of this book was made possible by funding from the Graham Foundation for the Advanced Studies in Fine Arts and the LEF Foundation. No part of this work covered by the copyright hereon may be reproduced or used in any form or by any means--graphic, electronic, or mechanical--without express written permission of the publisher. The publisher and the author assume no legal responsibility for the completeness or accuracy of the contents of this book.

Photographs by Julius Shulman: Drake's own house (pp. 14, 16, 17-8, 20-1), Spillman House(pp. 32-5), Presley House(pp. 37-41), Dammann House (pp. 42-5), the model of the Carmel studio (p. 49), the Malibu House (p. 2, 72-5), and Unit House (p. 6)
© 2011 by The J Paul Getty Museum, Los Angeles

Photographs by Morley Baer: Vacation House (pp. 53-7), Carmel Studio (pp. 58-61), Mesa house (pp. 19, 62-5), and Bayliss House (pp. 76-7).
© 2011 by the Morley Baer Photography Trust, Santa Fe

dust jacket and content design by Maliea Croy

Publishers Note

I am very pleased to re-print this book on Gordon Drake. It has always been one of my favorite books on California architecture and I have always prized the copy in my library. It is also an honor to have Glenn Murcutt take the time to write his introduction to this edition. Years ago Glenn ask me to find a copy of the Gordon Drake book for him and after much searching I did find a clean copy and sent it to him in Australia. It took time but he was very pleased. Glenn's book *Leaves Of Iron* by Philip Drew done in 1985 clarifies a similar approach to architecture as Gordon Drake. Upon reading it I realized Glenn's small practice was very similar to Gordon Drake's, where attention to detail and a love of the practice are very clear. Both in running a small practice did everything from original client contacts to finishing the building. Most impressive is the similar manner they completed the contract documents. Beautifully drawn sets of plans on a few sheets of vellum working out each detail. Often details done in isometrics to clarify a point.

A common thread Glenn and I have is our association with flying. Glenn above New Guinea in a Junker /31 + 34 and my father flying as a pilot in the U.S. Air Force. We saw a lot topography from the air. The Junker's were beautifully detailed airplanes skinned in corrugated metal.

. . .

I want to give a very special thanks also to Pierluigi Serraino who has pushed me over the years to get this book reprinted. His chapter brings new light to Gordon Drake's place in California architectural history. Pierluigi's special interest was the relationship Gordon had with Julius Shulman and how they worked together early in both of their careers supporting one another.

Also I want to thank Carrie McDade, Tony Watts, Lis Evans, Julie Cloutier, Bob Swatt, Victoria Shoemaker, Maliea Croy, Raj Shetty, Sarah Herda for offering insight and direction to the book.

Progressive Architecture

Effect of Building Materials on Design *Designs for a Church, Philippines: RAYMOND & RADO*	45
Structural *House, Los Angeles: GORDON DRAKE*	50
Surfacing *Public Hall, Clichy, France: BEAUDOIN & LODS*	57
Openings *Generator Building, Cambridge, Minn.: LONG & THORSHOV*	65
Insulation, Thermal and Acoustical *Theater, Long Beach, California: HUGH GIBBS* *Structural Insulating Material: DURISOL, Inc.*	69
Effect of Building Equipment on Design *Factory, Grand Rapids, Michigan: ALLEN & KELLEY*	74
Air and Temperature Control *House, Liverpool, N. Y.: SARGENT-WEBSTER-CRENSHAW & FOLLEY*	80
Lighting, Electrical *Store, Washington, D. C.: BERLA & ABEL*	86
Sanitation, Water Supply, Disposal *Lavatory, Chicago: GEORGE SENSENY, J. STEWART STEIN, Assoc.*	89
Specialized Equipment *Service Station, Los Angeles: WILLIAM F. HEMPEL*	91

EDITORIAL: 1   VIEWS: 8   PROGRESS REPORT: 14
MANUFACTURERS' LITERATURE: 96   REVIEWS: 100
JOBS AND MEN: 113   P.S.: 140

1/48

magazines with Drake articles

Progressive Architecture

6/48

Annual Progressive Architecture Awards	47
Jury Report, Class 1: DOUGLAS W. ORR	48
Award: ERNEST J. KUMP COMPANY	50
Class 1 Mentions:	51
ERNEST J. KUMP COMPANY; BUSH-BROWN & GAILEY, P. M. HEFFERNAN & R. L. AECK; ARTHUR FEHR & CHARLES GRANGER; ALONZO J. HARRIMAN, INC.; CARL L. MASTON; KETCHUM, GINA & SHARP; ROBERT LAW WEED & ASSOCIATES; CLYDE C. PEARSON & FARROW L. TITTLE, PARKER A. NARROWS & JOHN H. HANCOCK	
Jury Report, Class 2: DOUGLAS W. ORR	59
Class 2 Mentions:	60
FRANK GRUYS & L. E. McCONVILLE; GORDON DRAKE; E. H. & M. K. HUNTER; RAPHAEL S. SORIANO; KENNETH N. LIND; RUNNELLS, CLARK, WAUGH & MATSUMOTO; JOHN C. CAMPBELL & WORLEY K. WONG; JOHNSON & WHITCOMB	
Runners-Up	68
Office Practice: Your Legal Status During Construction	74
Sensible Detailing in Wood: HORNBOSTEL and TROUCHAUD	77
Fixturepanels: GUY G. ROTHENSTEIN	83
Selected Details: Store: Display Screen	91
House: Window	93
Office: Desk	95

EDITORIAL: 1 VIEWS: 8 PROGRESS REPORT: 14
PRODUCTS: 86 MANUFACTURERS' LITERATURE: 88
REVIEWS: 108 JOBS AND MEN: 124 P.S.: 152

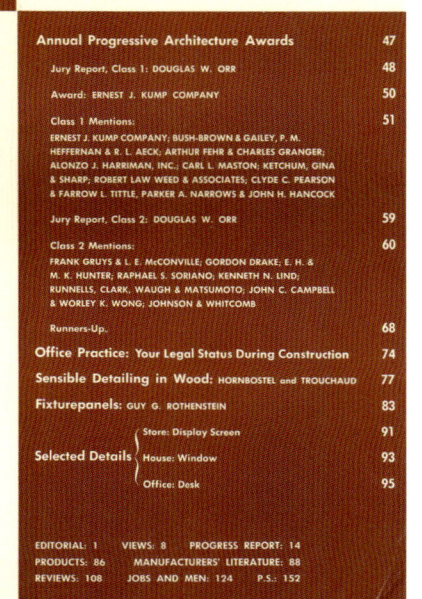

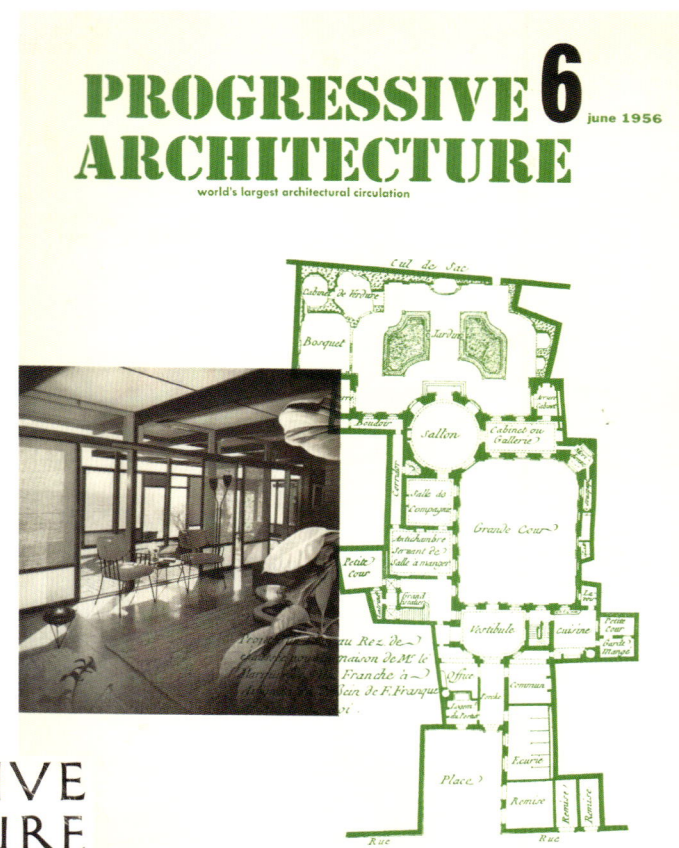

PROGRESSIVE ARCHITECTURE
6 june 1956
world's largest architectural circulation

p/a new house-to-site transition

PROGRESSIVE ARCHITECTURE

JUNE △ △ △ △ △ 1947

Advance Under Difficulties	
Progressive Architecture Award Winners and Citations:	53
KENNETH N. LIND for "California Cabin"	54
GORDON DRAKE for his own Home in Los Angeles	
WHITNEY R. SMITH for House in Pasadena, Calif.	56
ARTHUR T. BROWN for House in Tucson, Ariz.	
J. R. DAVIDSON for House in Los Angeles	57
MARCEL BREUER for House in Lawrence, Long Island	
E. H. and M. K. HUNTER for Showroom in Quechee, Vt.	58
ERNEST J. KUMP COMPANY for School in San Carlos, Calif.	
EBERLE M. SMITH ASSOCIATES for Health Center in Michigan	60
Drive-In Restaurant, Jantzen Beach, Ore.: PIETRO BELLUSCHI	61
Highway Restaurant, Baton Rouge, La.: A. HAYS TOWN	64
Pittsburgh in Progress: MITCHELL & RITCHEY	67
County and City Jail, Klamath Falls, Ore.: SHELDON BRUMBAUGH	73
Cape Cod Cottage, West Dennis, Mass.: DAVID FRIED	75
Welding: PAUL WEIDLINGER Part 1	79
Air Cleaning by Electronic Precipitation	84

VIEWS: 8 THIS MONTH: 14 PROGRESS REPORT: 20
PRODUCTS: 87 MANUFACTURERS' LITERATURE: 89
REVIEWS: 98 JOBS AND MEN: 114 OBSERVATIONS: 144

L'ARCHITECTURE D'AUJOURD'HUI
Nos 18-19 - JUIN 1948

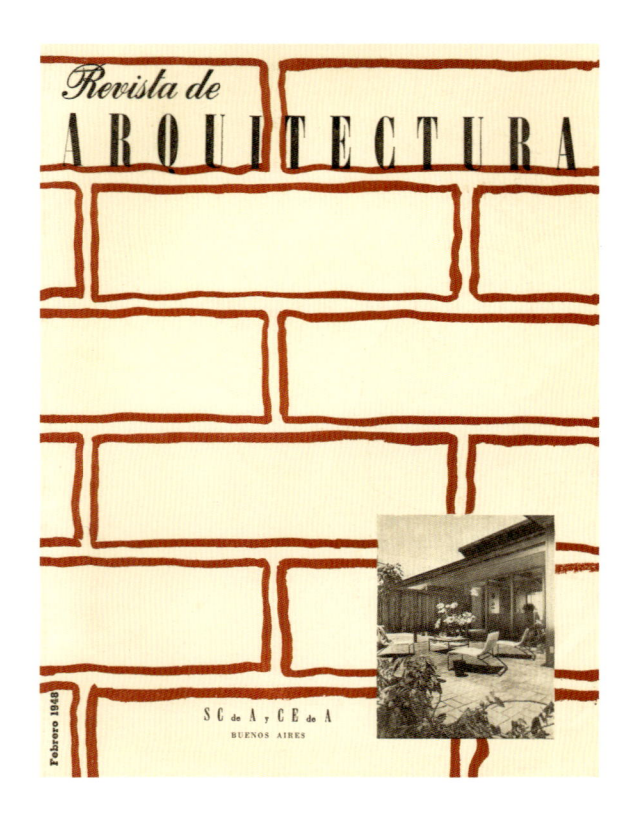

Revista de ARQUITECTURA
Febrero 1948
SC de A y CE de A
BUENOS AIRES

FORM 2 1947
SVENSKA
SLÖJDFÖRENINGENS
TIDSKRIFT

Revista de ARQUITECTURA
SC de A y CE de A
BUENOS AIRES
Noviembre 1947

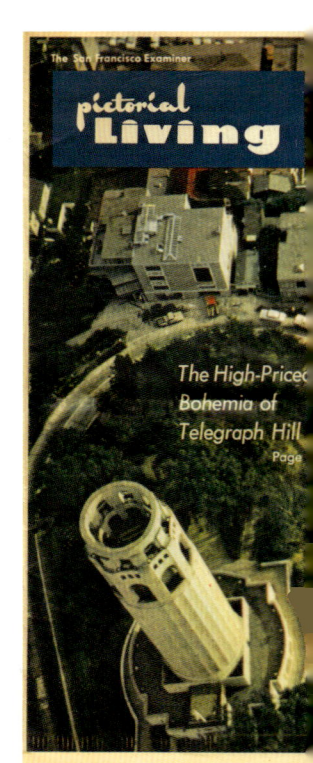

The San Francisco Examiner
pictorial Living
The High-Priced Bohemia of Telegraph Hill